W9-BVC-264

# Comin' Right at Ya

BRAD AND MICHELE MOORE ROOTS MUSIC SERIES

HOW A
JEWISH YANKEE HIPPIE
WENT COUNTRY, OR,
THE OFTEN OUTRAGEOUS
HISTORY OF
ASLEEP AT THE
WHEEL

AND
DAVID MENCONI

UNIVERSITY OF TEXAS PRESS
AUSTIN

Copyright © 2015 by Ray Benson
All rights reserved
Printed in the United States of America
First edition, 2015

Requests for permission to reproduce
material from this work should be sent to:
Permissions
University of Texas Press
P.O. Box 7819
Austin, TX 78713-7819
http://utpress.utexas.edu/index.php/rp-form

The paper used in this book meets the minimum requirements of
ANSI/NISO Z39.48-1992 (R1997) (Permanence of Paper). ∞

LIBRARY OF CONGRESS CATALOGING DATA
Benson, Ray, 1951- author.
Comin' right at ya : how a Jewish Yankee hippie went country, or, the
often outrageous history of Asleep at the Wheel / Ray Benson
and David Menconi. — First edition.
pages cm — (Brad and Michele Moore roots music series)
Includes index.
ISBN 978-0-292-75658-8 (cloth)
ISBN 978-1-4773-0773-1 (library e-book)
ISBN 978-1-4773-0774-8 (non-library e-book)
1. Benson, Ray, 1951- 2. Asleep at the Wheel (Musical group) 3. Country
musicians—United States—Biography. 4. Western swing (Music)
5. Popular music—Texas. I. Menconi, David, author. II. Title.
III. Series: Brad and Michele Moore roots music series.
ML420.B34397A3 2015
781.642092'2—dc23
2015002176

doi:10.7560/756588

# Contents

# Prologue

## FEBRUARY 15, 1979

INTO EACH LIFE some thankless gigs must fall. And let me tell you, brothers and sisters, I've played plenty over the past forty-some years with Asleep at the Wheel—not just thankless but depressing, crazy, weird, catastrophic, and even some all-of-the-above combination of supremely bad mojo. I've gone through breakdowns of everything imaginable, from transportation to gear to poor, fragile psyches. And I've had people up and quit on me in mid-gig, onstage as well as in the audience.

In good time, we shall get to all of it. But let me begin by telling you about the most memorably bad gig of my career, a best-of-times, worst-of-times little affair that happened on a cold and windy Sunday night a long time ago in the fair city of Lubbock, Texas.

There's a scene in my stage show *A Ride with Bob* where I ask the ghost of Bob Wills what heaven's like, and he talks about how the souls of the departed "watch the whole world go by without us" from up in the clouds. To which I crack, "Sounds like Lubbock." Yeah, I'm a funny guy, even if Lubbock's city fathers might not agree. But I kid 'cause I care, and any town that gave us Buddy Holly, the Maines family, and most of the Flatlanders can't be all bad even if there ain't much to do there besides study for an engineering degree at Texas Tech.

Anyway: Lubbock, Ides of February, 1979. The wind was blowing in Lubbock that night because it always does, and Asleep at the Wheel was booked into a joint there called 8 Second Ride, so named for how long you have to stay on top of a rodeo ride. On our side of the stage, the gig itself went pretty well because (as the late great Hunter S. Thompson used to say) we are professionals, after all. We got there on time, more or less, and played a good set. But the problem was that nobody—I mean, NOBODY—showed up to hear us. Well, a few people were there; an eight-person "crowd" at the 8 Second Ride. We played for an empty room that was colder than a prison guard's stare.

Crickets, and not the kind that used to back up Buddy Holly. Good times.

It's possible nobody came to our show that night because they were all at home watching the Grammy Awards on television, which is kind of what I wish I'd been doing. Our recording of the Count Basie classic "One O'Clock Jump" was up for Best Country Instrumental (and can I just say how proud it makes me to be lead vocalist of an ensemble so consistently honored for instrumental performances?), which was the sixth time we'd been nominated. The ceremonies were happening in Los Angeles, with John Denver hosting. But we didn't go because we figured we had no shot, never having won for any of our prior nominations. Plus we were flat broke, as always, so we chose to spend that weekend playing shows and trying to make some money.

And how'd that work out? Glad you asked. After we gutted it out for that handful of frozen, hostile crickets in Lubbock, end of the night came and it was time to settle up. The club owner pleaded poverty—uh-huh, cry me a river, dude.

"Let me tell you about that," I said. "Poverty is dragging ass four hundred miles up here to play for a $3,000 guarantee. Which we did. And you're going to pay us—now."

Sometimes it helps to be six-foot-seven.

So with much grumbling, the club owner set to raiding his waitresses' tip jars and even emptying quarters out of the pool tables to try to come up with enough to pay us our guarantee. It was an ugly and depressing scene, me and the rest of the band holding vigil on the bus while our road manager went back and forth to report on how it was going—"Well, we're almost there . . ."—leaving us to wonder how the hell we were going to cover next week's bills if it came up short.

In the midst of this disaster, some guy none of us knew ran onto the bus and hollered, "Hey! Y'all just won a Grammy!! I heard it on the news!!!"

No way. We looked at the guy like he was out of his damn mind. But just in case he wasn't insane or pranking us, we turned on the TV and found a station doing the news. Sure enough, the recap of that night's Grammy winners included "Austin's Asleep at the Wheel in the category of Best Country Instrumental." Well, now, how about that?

We came home to backslaps and a nice telegram from the president of Capitol Records, who wished us "congratulations on your well-deserved Grammy." A week or two later, our actual Grammy statues showed up in the mail. Had our name stamped on them and everything, which was cool. That didn't stop our fiddle player, Danny Levin, from using the gramophone on his for an ashtray. And Chris O'Connell, Asleep at the Wheel's girl singer for fifteen years and my on-again-off-again girlfriend (sometimes both at the same time) had the nameplate fall off of hers almost immediately.

Chris has always had the voice of an angel, but back then, she also had a wicked taste for cognac that sometimes got out of hand. One of those nights came around where she got tanked and we started going at it, and she got mad enough to take my Grammy and chuck it at me. She missed, but the damn thing broke in two. I had to get a jeweler to repair it. It's back in one piece now, although you can still see the crack—just like the Liberty Bell.

Figures, me being from Philadelphia and all. But it's still on my shelf, and it still counts.

Looking back all these years later, that first Grammy came at a pivotal moment in Asleep at the Wheel's history, although not in the way I was hoping at the time. Finally winning a Grammy made us feel like we really were a legit part of showbiz, and that was the first of nine we would win—a right nice sum, thank ya very much, and I hope we're not done yet. By early 1979, the band had been together for almost a decade and those first years were so tough that nobody in their right mind would have put up with it (fortuitously, none of us were in our right mind, then or now).

Even though we'd had a few hits, country radio never exactly took to Asleep at the Wheel, being that we were a little more countercultural than what it was used to, while playing the sort of old-school honky-tonk music that was decidedly out of favor in the country mainstream. "We can't play your record on the radio because it sounds like 1940"—we heard things like that over and over. While that didn't stop us from doing things our way, it did mean that we were just barely getting by. I remember hoping that the prestige of winning a Grammy might make things a little less tight.

We couldn't have known it, but Asleep at the Wheel was on the verge of entering a lean period that would whittle us down to skin and bones. Trends were running against us even more than usual. The music industry beyond Nashville was disco-crazed in the late 1970s, as everybody chased after the next *Saturday Night Fever*. Two-stepping to "Cotton Eye Joe" was out, gettin' down to "Love to Love You Baby" was in.

A few years later, after the movie *Urban Cowboy* made redneck joints fashionable, the same nightclubs that had quit hiring live bands in favor of disco deejays were switching out their disco balls for mechanical bull rides. Yee-haw! But just our luck, we managed to miss that boat, too. Asleep at the Wheel actually had an offer to be in *Urban Cowboy* with John Travolta, but we opted to do *Roadie* with Meat Loaf instead because it was being made by some friends of ours. Seemed like a good idea at the time, but *Roadie* would gross about one-tenth of what *Urban Cowboy* did. Who knew?

Getting back to the promised land would take most of the '80s, and all my wiles. Asleep at the Wheel spent the better part of that decade without a record deal, teetering on the edge of bankruptcy as the band's lineup turned into a revolving door. We didn't win our second Grammy until 1988, and in between fell a hardscrabble period that I still don't know how we survived. But, hell, I was used to that. Still am. It's probably why my pal Willie Nelson calls me a "street hustler"—because I've had to be.

Asleep at the Wheel started out as a bunch of college friends on a quest, and while we did have some lofty (and naive) ideas about being accepted as a working-class country band, there never was anything like a long-term plan. It was always close to the bone, figuring out how to get from one gig to the next. When you've got a twelve-piece band on the road, it's hard to contemplate much more than the latest bridge you're about to jump off of.

About a hundred people have passed through Asleep at the Wheel over the years, which isn't really that many when you think about it. Twelve-piece band that's been around more than forty years—you do the math. People have left, retired, even died. But most who left did so because we play a very specific kind of music that people maybe don't want to spend their entire careers playing. Maybe that's why Asleep at the Wheel has been sort of like a catch-and-release talent incubator, with a bunch of people coming through and going on to play with Bob Dylan, Willie Nelson, George Strait, Waylon Jennings, Lyle Lovett, Merle Haggard, Shania Twain, Alabama, Ryan Adams, and a lot more.

Not me, though. I've stayed with the Asleep at the Wheel finishing school all these years while also producing records, TV shows, and commercials, acting in movies, doing voice-over work, running a studio. Keeping a lot of irons in the fire is a must, and I do. But leading the band has always been my main thing, and it always will be. For better or worse, I'm still the kid mugging for the camera: "Hey! Here I am!!"

Sometimes it's worked out in unexpected ways because we never knew who was out there listening, or how they'd take it. A fellow named Pete Finney once told me he saw us open for Alice Cooper and Hot Tuna in 1970, and it changed his life—set him on the path and inspired him to take up steel guitar. Eventually, he became Patty Loveless's steel player and an in-demand session guy in Nashville. Asleep at the Wheel opened a lot of ears and eyes over the years.

It's been a circuitous route. We started out in 1970 in Paw Paw, West Virginia, playing for hillbillies there and hipsters in Washington, D.C., before moving to California; got Nashville's attention while backing up semi-famous country singers; moved to Texas just in time to be part of the mid-'70s outlaw-country thing with Waylon and Willie and the boys; survived disco (barely); had a few mainstream country hits in the late '80s and started winning Grammys; and hit our stride in the '90s as America's preeminent modern-day Western swing band carrying on the sound and style of our kindred spirit Bob Wills. Asleep at the Wheel has done three Wills tribute albums, but in a way everything we do is a tribute to him.

I've always played retro music that's out of step with the mainstream, but that hasn't kept me from being ahead of the curve on a lot of things. Seems like I always get there before someone was famous or something was hip, and not just with music. When I was a kid growing up in Philadelphia, one of my early playmates from the neighborhood was a foreign-exchange student named Ben—you might know him nowadays as Benjamin Netanyahu, prime minister of Israel.

In 1963, I was twelve years old and my family was visiting England, and I got to see the Beatles six months before Beatlemania came to America. In 1971, when Asleep at the Wheel was still based in West Virginia, we were hanging out one night in Washington, D.C., with a duo called Fat City, and they played us something they'd just written for a still-unknown singer-songwriter. It made me laugh, a song likening West Virginia to "almost heaven"—but John Denver did okay with "Take Me Home, Country Roads." A few years later, a guy at our record company told us,

"We've got another act like you guys, sells well in Texas and New Jersey. We haven't figured out how to get him, or you, out to a wider audience." While they never did figure us out, they did fine with that other guy, Bruce Springsteen.

George Strait, Garth Brooks, Vince Gill, Lyle Lovett, Kacey Musgraves, and countless others opened for us on their way up. For some of them, like George, I'd like to think we helped pave their way. You know what they say about pioneers taking all the arrows, but it's worked out just fine. There were times when getting there first had some advantages. We got to be the very first band to play *Austin City Limits* (after Willie did the pilot, of course), episode number one in 1976. Been back there a bunch, too.

Looking back as my career closes in on the half-century mark, I wouldn't change a thing. Well, except for mistakes I've made and some dumb-ass things other people have done. Take those out of the equation, and it probably would've been a smoother ride. But a less interesting one, too. I was probably destined for the hard road.

Whatever anyone else wants to say about me, I'm just about the least likely success story there is. Asleep at the Wheel is a Texas institution, and I guess that makes me one, too, since I'm the only one who's been there the whole time. I've always said that Asleep at the Wheel has to change to go on and that the band is bigger than any one individual—yours truly excepted, of course. One monkey don't stop no show, unless it's this monkey. I may not be larger than life, but I fill it up pretty good, Texas-style, which is funny considering that I grew up in Pennsylvania going to synagogue. But if a Jewish guy from Philadelphia can reinvent himself as a country-western star from Texas, what could be a better example of how the American dream is alive and well? Or, as my buddy Terry Allen once put it in a song:

*Gone to Texas*
*All I need is the ride . . .*

Dream it, be it, follow your bliss. And if you keep at it long enough, maybe catch a break or two, you never know what fate might throw your way. A quarter century after Asleep at the Wheel won that first Grammy Award, I was appointed "Official Texas State Musician" of 2004, an honor that has also gone to Willie Nelson, Flaco Jiménez, ZZ Top's Billy Gibbons, and other native sons over the years.

Then in 2011, the 170th Texas Legislature up and declared me, Ray Benson—real name Ray Seifert, a Jewish Yankee born and raised seventeen hundred miles and five states north of Austin—"Texan of the Year." House Resolution 844, which somehow passed unanimously. That also gave me the juice to get a burial plot in the Texas State Cemetery (a place reserved for legislators and "significant Texans"), where I will someday be laid to rest alongside Bud Shrake, Ann Richards, Sam Houston, Tom Landry, and other notables.

It was a tremendous honor that left me deeply, deeply humbled, but also amused and confused. I found myself asking the same question, then and now:

*How the hell did I get here?*

Hell if I know, but let's find out.

# Friday's Child

ACCORDING TO A well-worn family story, after I was born and my mom woke up, she asked to see her baby. They brought her a small olive-skinned newborn from the hospital nursery.

"This is not mine!" my mom screamed, and off they ran to find the right baby. That would be me.

I was born in the early-morning hours of March 16, 1951, a Friday. Always thought I should've shown up either a day earlier, since Thursday's child "has far to go" (no doubt) or a day later, because Saturday's child "works hard for a living" (and ain't *that* the truth). But, nope, I got Friday, which makes me "loving and giving." I guess it was inevitable that I'd wind up a slow-moving hippie.

But I sure did start out in a hurry, born a month premature, my back all arched instead of being rolled up in the usual fetal position because, the doctor said, I really wanted to get out. Even as an early arrival, I was good-sized and tipped the scales at seven pounds, six ounces. Since I came out the hard way, I was black and blue all over—face battered and bruised, nose sticking off to the side, ears misplaced, all topped off by a shock of red hair. I looked like I'd been on the losing end of a twelve-round championship bout decided by technical knockout, and Mom freaked out all over again.

“Don’t worry,” the doctor reassured her. “His ears will go back to where they’re supposed to be . . . well, someday.” Eventually, they did. But all that commotion probably explains why I’ve had so many weird, recurrent birthing dreams over the years. Hard to remember many specifics beyond the fact that they’re loud and involve lots of roaring, crazy shit. A fitting beginning, I’d say.

Once I’d made my entrance into the world, my early years were fairly sedate. I was born Ray Benson Seifert, named after my just-deceased grandmother Rae (short for Rachel), and I was the third of four children in a family of modest working-class means in Philadelphia. Big brother Mike kicked off the Seifert baby boom in 1947, followed by big sister Sandy in 1949, then me in 1951, with my little brother Hank bringing up the rear in 1955.

My earliest memory is being four years old and seeing my mom’s big pregnant belly. Then she left for a few days and came home, without the big belly but with Hank. It will surprise no one who knows me that I’m a middle child. Yes, I’m hard-wired to crave attention. And everybody in the Seifert family is on the tall side, but I’m the tallest by far and also have the biggest feet (try some 16 EEE shoes on for size and then let me know where you found ’em, because shoes that big are just about impossible to find). I think I willed myself to be this big. Robert Plant once said of me, “Ray Benson is one of the few people I look up to, and I have no choice.”

After my arrival, the growing Seifert clan moved to Whitemarsh Village, a subdivision that, like many developments built right after World War II, had a lot of thoroughfares named after Patton, MacArthur, Marshall, and other American generals. The neighborhood was on the grounds of this huge old mansion built by turn-of-the-century robber barons as a replica of the Palace of Versailles in France, with gardens, statues, and fountains. There were fences, but we knew how to get through, so we spent a lot of time roaming the grounds on weekends and after business hours, traipsing through the woods and catching creatures while pretending to be Davy Crockett. My childhood was a very idealized *Leave It to Beaver* kind of world. Since we were allowed to watch only thirty minutes of television a night, we did stuff.

The family homestead was 1201 Claridge Road, a three-bedroom house at the corner of Claridge and Hull Drive. Cost my dad $12,500 through the GI Bill in 1951. Michael and I shared a room, which we plastered with pictures cut out of *Sports Illustrated* magazine—Wilt Chamberlain and other Philadelphia sports icons, various Phillies, Eagles, and Flyers. Chuck Bednarik, the last two-way player in the NFL, lived down the street from us. It was the days before million-dollar sports contracts, and he made $6,000 a year playing both offense and defense for the Eagles, center and linebacker. So he ran a cement business in the off-season.

During my wonder years, we also spent a lot of time on a houseboat my dad had bought for us to spend summers on—except it spent more time in our side yard than on the water. The boat's hull had holes, and rather than weld them shut, my dad had the bright idea of filling the hull with polyurethane. You might know that as Styrofoam, which floats but also absorbs water. So after a summer where we spent more time bailing than sailing, the boat came back to the house and sat there rotting for years. It became the kids' clubhouse. Great place to smoke dope, too, because the mildew covered up the smell.

I grew up thinking we were poor because my parents were saving all their money for us kids to go to college. My family was solidly Jewish immigrant, not too many generations removed from the Old World. Both sets of grandparents had escaped Eastern Europe for America around 1900, fleeing the pogroms, and my father, Maurice "Maury" Seifert, was born in South Philly in 1914.

While my dad wouldn't have called himself a musician, he loved to play piano and sing, holding court and entertaining at gatherings. Those were his stages, and he was the life of every party, outgoing and gregarious—and related to me, what are the odds? He loved to laugh and he loved to talk, as do all the

Seiferts, me most of all. I had a guy ask me on the golf course once if I used sunblock on my tongue (hmm, not a bad idea). My dad and I would butt heads repeatedly during my teenage years because we were a lot alike—both of us stubborn.

My dad served in the military during World War II, but he was injured in a training accident. Then he did one year at Drexel studying mechanical engineering before setting up shop as a businessman-inventor and small-time industrialist. He owned Seifert Machinery Company and Dumatic Industries in Philadelphia, making machines that labeled cigarettes or toothbrushes or whatever else as they moved down the conveyor belt.

Just like me, my dad was a retro guy. He made mechanical things with cams, gears, cogs, and wheels turning, which started to become obsolete in the 1960s because of electronics. But my dad never really changed with the times. He kept it old-school, and it seemed like every person he ever hired at Seifert Machinery Company had a foreign accent. Years later, I learned they were all refugees from the 1956 Hungarian Revolution who had fled the Communist takeover and come to America. They were the best tool-and-die guys in the world, really knew how to make machines.

Despite his company's growing obsolescence, Dad had chances to sell out to bigger manufacturers. But he never did. When we kids got to be old enough to ask why, our parents explained that Dad hung on to his business because being the boss allowed him to take summers off to go on big trips with us. And we were travelin' fools.

In 1958, my dad bought a brand-new Volkswagen Microbus and built a platform across the back so all six of us could lie down and sleep in it. Over the next few years, we went to California (where we got one of the first hula hoops ever made, before they became a nationwide craze), Florida, Canada, all over New England. We drove Route 66, Highway 40, out to the West, down South, and every other direction. This was pre-interstate America, so we were on a lot of two-lane blacktops. My dad would hear about a shortcut at the gas-station counter, get directions, and go.

It was great preparation for my future life.

Some of those family vacations were for business, like a 1963 trip we took to Europe so my dad could sell some labeling machines. That was a formative experience, meeting cousins around Europe. When we didn't have relatives to stay with, we roughed it and camped out in tents. We brought along our guitars, too, and played with all sorts of foreigners. They seemed to know all the same folk songs we did, so language barriers were seldom a problem.

Eighteen years after World War II, lots of Europe was still torn up and seemed primitive compared to America. Milk wasn't pasteurized; it was boiled and tasted horrible to the point of rotten. And because gas was super-expensive, everybody seemed to travel either on bicycles or in itty-bitty cars that looked like they'd fit inside a suitcase. For someone raised on the tailfins of huge American sedans, it was as foreign as foreign could be.

Being Jewish, we had to go visit some of the old World War II concentration camps, which was scary. In Belgium, we met some cousins in their twenties who told us about hiding from the Nazis in caves for so long that they got rickets from lack of sunlight. And we also met some Germans who still didn't have a lick of shame about the whole thing. I remember my dad getting into an argument with this one old German guy who actually said, "You should thank us for stopping the Communists from overrunning Europe." I guess that was the German Army's story and they were sticking to it. While they were at it, too bad they didn't stop the Russians from overrunning the other half of Europe.

Years later, in the 1980s, Asleep at the Wheel did a cultural-exchange tour where we played behind the Iron Curtain. We played in Czechoslovakia, and we were too stupid to realize we couldn't take the Czech money they paid us with out of the country. Well, they make nice cut glass over there, so I bought some for my mom.

I remember sitting in a backstage room with a Romanian country band. I had a guitar pick I didn't like, threw it down, and they asked if they could have it. Sure thing. We got to talking, and they told me it cost them a week's salary to get a set of guitar strings (and here I thought the music business in America was tough). That's where I learned why communism doesn't work: you couldn't just make something, like guitar strings, unless the state let you.

In the UK on that 1963 trip, we stayed with my cousins in Bath, a resort town in the south of England. They were into music, and they were particularly keen on one band from up north.

"There's this group you simply must see," they told us. "They'll be on the telly today."

It was a show called *Juke Box Jury*, and my first thought about this band was that they had the weirdest haircuts I'd ever seen. All us American kids had greaser haircuts with Brylcreem, but the Beatles were proud to let their shaggy hair fly. I didn't think much about them until about six months later, when they were on *The Ed Sullivan Show* in America—"Wait a minute, those are the same guys I saw over in England last year!"

The next day I went into math class with my hair combed over and down, just like every other adolescent male in the United States. But I managed to get thrown out of class.

Apart from Europe, probably our most memorable trip was one we took in 1958, after my dad designed a machine that shoved Marlboros into crush-proof cigarette boxes. He took us along on a journey to demonstrate it to some cigarette companies in Tobacco Town, otherwise known as Winston-Salem, North Carolina. It would be eye-opening in all the wrong ways.

I was seven years old, and that was my first time way down south, which meant it was my first exposure to institutional racism below the Mason-Dixon Line. My parents were pretty free-spirited for that time, basically New Deal liberals who hated Joe McCarthy and his "Red Scare" stuff. So I was unprepared for the Jim Crow South and its "whites only" signs on buses, bathrooms, and water fountains.

I saw a chain gang of black men watched over by white armed guards as they broke rocks, which scared the living hell out of me. And I couldn't believe how tiny the shotgun shacks were, or how many kids were crammed into each one.

Even at that age, I could tell that segregation just wasn't right.

You could say my parents bookended World War I—you know, the first (but not last) War to End All Wars. My father was born in 1914, the year it started, and my mother was born in May of the year it ended. They met in their early twenties at one of the Catskills "Borscht Belt" resorts where generations of Jewish families took summer vacations and courted each other.

My mom's given name was Pearl, but everybody called her Bobby; she was the baby of the family, youngest of five kids. That didn't make her childhood any easier. My mom never knew her own father because he died in the 1918 flu pandemic three months before she was born, so she grew up in a single-parent family. Somehow they all excelled through the Great Depression, especially Bobby.

My mom was an amazing, brilliant woman who worked her way through Temple University and got a master's degree at the University of Pennsylvania while raising four kids. After college, she was a public-school teacher in Philadelphia starting in 1943. She taught fourth grade at Brook Elementary, and one of her students was Wilt Chamberlain, on his way to becoming a seven-foot-one-inch basketball giant. But my mom didn't remember him, so (unlike yours truly) he must not have been causing too much trouble. In 1970, she went to work for one of the first Head Start programs, trying to get inner-city kids to read. She wrote textbooks, too. Incredible woman. When she was ninety, they gave her two weeks to live, and she lived another two years before passing in 2010. Never could sing a lick until the end of her life, after having a stroke. I was visiting her, playing some songs, and suddenly she could sing along in tune.

If my gregarious side comes from my dad, then I picked up whatever bleeding-heart humanitarian tendencies I have from my mom. An enlightened liberal and activist, she ran for the school board. While I was growing up, the McCarthy hearings, civil rights, and peace marches dominated dinner-table discussions. Then when I was in fifth grade, she got a job at Miquon, an alternative school where teachers who'd been blacklisted by McCarthy went to work.

I got to go to Miquon for two years, too, and that place liberated me. In public school, I'd always been in trouble. My fourth-grade teacher loved my older brother and sister (who were both admittedly brilliant) but declared me to be a problem.

"You need to make Ray sit in a chair without moving for an hour every night," she told my mom. "Tie him down if you have to."

There was none of that at Miquon, where you could call teachers by their first name and wear jeans. It encouraged creative thinking rather than the by-rote, disciplinary bullshit of public school, and I thrived there. Even when I went back to public school in seventh grade, I still made straight A's. Then in eighth grade, they put in advanced-placement classes and I backslid in a hurry. The problem was that I've always had attention deficit disorder (ADD), which I think is more of a personality trait than a disability. But all the things that go with that just didn't work in school. I was a difficult child, way too smart and way too undisciplined for anyone to handle. Seemed like whenever a teacher called on me, I'd be looking out the window, daydreaming and writing a poem in my head.

"You're under-achieving," they kept telling me. "We know you can do better if you'd just apply yourself."

True enough. But school just wasn't interesting enough to overcome my short attention span. Fortunately, by then I was into something else that was.

# You Get a Smile Every Time with the Heads-up Taste of a Ballantine

I STARTED TRYING to whistle at about age four, so I guess that's when making music started for me. My big brother, Mike, played saxophone and clarinet, which I would do my best to imitate by whistling. Then came playing recorder in the obligatory first-grade music class, followed by several years of piano lessons. One of my few regrets is not keeping that up even though the basketball coach wanted me to because, he said, playing piano would be good for my hands. Oh well.

Then at age nine, I found the exact right instrument—the first time I picked up a guitar, tried to play it, and discovered I already knew how. Not that I was a virtuoso prodigy or anything, but I could play right away, no sweat. It was my sister's four-string guitar, which she was taking lessons on, and from the start I could pick out enough notes to get by. First thing I fumbled my way through was the tune to the beer jingle I heard over and over during commercial breaks for the Phillies games I listened to on my pink-ish transistor radio. Single note, easy to play, and I still remember it word for word all these years later:

*To be crisp a beer must be icily light*
*With true lively flavor precisilly right*
*The crisp refresher*
*(the crisp refresher)*

*Ballantine, Ballantine Beer! . . .*
*You get a smile every time*
*With the heads-up taste of a Ballantine!*

From there, I moved on to the Carter Family's "Wildwood Flower" and Elizabeth Cotten's "Freight Train" (the first two fingerpicking songs I learned) along with "This Land Is Your Land," "On Top of Old Smokey," and the other folk songs you'd hear on the radio back then. The folk tunes that crossed over to pop were like a beginning-guitar primer. Mother Maybelle Carter's picking was easy to figure out and a lot simpler than what Merle Travis did, which was something I had to work up to.

But the radio was a great teacher. It might be hard to fathom in this age of specialized niches, but back then you'd hear everything from the Ventures to Patsy Cline on pop radio. James Brown was on there right alongside Buddy Holly, the Ronettes segueing into the Everly Brothers, Chubby Checker bumping up against Frank Sinatra. You could get a hell of an education just from spinning the dial. I listened on my little radio, and I took a crack at playing a little of this, a little of that, and a lot of the other.

I started buying records, starting with a 45 of Fats Domino's "Walking to New Orleans." The first album I ever got was one by Pete Seeger, and the second was by Barbra Streisand (how am I not gay?). At some point, too, my cousin from New York sent us an old wire recorder that had been lying around his uncle's apartment. When I turned it on, I heard Big Bill Broonzy singing "Stagger Lee."

Oh yeah, welcome home.

I started accompanying Sandy to her guitar lessons over at a friend's house, and I took a few lessons myself. But mostly I learned guitar on my own from trading licks with other people. Once I got started playing, it didn't take long for me to make the jump to the stage. Sandy was in a group called the Three G's (Guys, Girls, and Guitars), which became the Four G's when I joined at age ten. We'd play in matching uniforms ordered out of a Sears catalog—square-dance outfits for the girls and denim shirts with beige chinos for the guys, plus light-green Hush Puppies and white socks for everyone. Let me tell ya, we were *cute*.

My first public performances for crowds were with the Four G's, so I guess you'd say that's where I found my place. From the start, I loved being onstage. Never had stage fright. Some people get almost paralyzed with fear, but, man, getting onstage is what I'm always working toward because I love being in front of people and talking and singing. What really put the hook in for good was playing for five thousand people with the Philadelphia Orchestra, doing "On Top of Old Smokey" and "This Land Is Your Land." The energy from being in front of that many people was amazing. By the time we were halfway through the first verse, I was hooked.

Ever see *A Mighty Wind*, Christopher Guest's very funny 2003 "mockumentary" comedy about the '50s and '60s folk revival? I lived that. The Four G's were part of the folk era before Beatlemania, with acts like the Kingston Trio, the Clancy Brothers, and Peter, Paul, and Mary on the radio. There were a lot of folk clubs and coffeehouses like the Second Fret around Philadelphia, but we just played the "safe" places like youth centers and school talent shows. My mom, our biggest fan and protector, was always advising me on how to work a crowd.

"Before each song," she told me once, "you need to tell the audience a little something about it." That was how I learned stage patter, an invaluable onstage survival skill. I didn't know it, but I was being groomed for show business.

The Four G's were just one part of my early musical education, a lot of which took place in various orchestras and jazz groups playing Bach, Vivaldi, bossa nova jazz. Later, in the eighth grade, I also took up bass fiddle at the suggestion of my mom, who remembered from dating musicians that bands are always looking for a bass player (good advice). Tuba followed a year later; I took lessons from Abe Torchinsky of the Philadelphia Orchestra and played sousaphone in the marching band because I could handle it better than most, thanks to my size. Somewhere in there, I also found time to sing in the choir. I think it's worth noting that a lot of this happened at school. To those who think that music isn't an important part of education, I'm here to say: You're wrong.

Looking back now, all of that sounds like it was a little manic, and I guess it was. But within all the music I played, I was finding connective threads I wouldn't even be aware of until much later.

Around the time I turned fourteen years old, in 1965, the Four G's came to an end. The last thing I remember us doing before breaking up was this folk-festival hootenanny sponsored by a new beverage called Mountain Dew—which was bright green, heavily caffeinated, and came in a can with what looked like a drunk hillbilly on it. They even had a song about Mountain Dew for us to sing, which went like this, near as I can remember:

*They call it the good ol' Mountain Dew*
*Them's that refuse it are few*
*If you hush up your mug*
*I'll fill up your jug*
*With good ol' Mountain Dew.*

Pure poetry, I tell ya.

Beatlemania coming to America the year before had been the beginning of the end of folk music for me, so I could not have cared less about the Four G's breaking up. Besides which, I was plenty busy elsewhere by then, and not just with all that square school-band shit. I had already met one of my future partners in crime, Reuben Gosfield, when we were both about three years old. Reuben's family lived two doors down from one of my Four G's bandmates, and his mom and dad were like second parents to me, so I was over at their house a lot.

My mom and dad may have been open-minded, but Reuben's parents were beatniks (albeit suburban beatniks, with four kids), and I cannot tell you how unimaginably cool that was for a fourteen-year-old. They had an old record player with some even older jazz and blues 78's. Reuben got me into the blues, which added Muddy Waters and Howlin' Wolf to my palette just about the time I got my first electric guitar.

It was a Harmony, a cheap Gibson 335 knockoff I ordered out of the Montgomery Ward catalog and paid for with money I'd made lifeguarding at day camp over the summer. I didn't have an amplifier, so I had to improvise: I hooked it up to an old tape recorder of my dad's because the plug from the guitar cord just happened to fit, and the sound came out distorted as all hell—but it was on, baby, on. Loud, too.

Reuben had a guitar of his own and so we started jamming, which naturally led to the formation of terrible garage bands. We started a whole series of short-lived bands that might play a gig or two at a party or teen center before giving way to the next group. One was called the Red Eye Blues Band. Another I remember from a few years later was a psychedelic blues band called Orange Juice. I wrote the songs, such as they were. There was "Art Student Dilemma 1" (which begat a sequel, "Art Student Dilemma 2"). And also "Orange Juice," which was code for acid.

*Orange juice is good for you*
*Orange juice is refreshing and new . . .*

Don't know why we weren't all over the radio.

Being a big kid, I also played just about every sport there was all through school—baseball, golf, tennis, even some soccer. I played football briefly, until I realized I just didn't like the head-knocking part of it. Before that, I played two years of Pee Wee football; the team picture from 1962 was adorable. And basketball, of course, since I was so tall. My position was power forward, but I'd jump center because I had good ups—I could dunk at age fifteen. So of course they outlawed it the next year.

Bastards. All the more reason to stick with music.

My big sister, Sandy, was obviously an important musical influence with the Four G's, and she was the glue that held the Seifert family together. She married her husband, Gerry, when they were both teenagers, and they taught school for thirty-eight years. Because she stayed in Philadelphia, care of our parents in their old age fell to her (my dad would pass on in 2001, a month shy of his eighty-seventh birthday). Sandy handled it with far more grace than I could have managed.

As for my little brother, Hank, he was my playmate growing up, which meant he basically served as my tackling dummy. We'd play one-on-one tackle football for hours, and I'd just cream him. I'm not proud to say I was Hank's torturer for many years, to the point that I felt the need to apologize much, much later. I'll do it again here: Sorry, Hank. But given that you're the Seifert family's first and only Ph.D. and you teach genetic microbiology at Northwestern Medical School, I couldn't have hurt ya too bad. You make me proud, buddy.

But my big brother, Mike, left the biggest mark of all. Mike was four years older than me, and a hero to all of us. Growing up, I wanted to beat him at everything more than anything. Whether it was games or sports or school, I never could. Took the SAT test and did great, 668 and 669. Mike was over 700 on both. It was always like that.

Still, I couldn't be mad at Mike, because he let me hang out with him and his friends. He also gave me his Vespa motor scooter when he went off to college. It was the perfect mode of transportation for a fourteen-year-old; a dime's worth of gas, and I could go all day. Used to drive myself and Hank to school on it, too, and I freaked out a date's parents by showing up on it once. Dunno why they were worried. It's not like we could have had sex on the back of it.

Mike lived life to the fullest even though it dealt him a tough hand. At age nineteen, he was diagnosed with syringomyelia—a rare degenerative disease that also killed golfer Bobby Jones. Mike had paralysis setting in by the time he was in his twenties, a gradual atrophy that started from the fingertips and eventually reached his respiratory system. But for most of his life, it barely slowed him down. He got a philosophy degree at Oberlin, to the bafflement of our father.

"Where can you get a job philosophizing?" Maury asked. I don't know, but Mike wound up as a technical writer for computer software and did fine.

Eventually, the disease took over, and Mike was completely paralyzed for his last few years. He was in and out of consciousness toward the end; but when he was in, he was in. I remember visiting during his hospice period and asking if he wanted a joint.

"Nah, man," he said. "I got *way* better shit than that!"

Mike died in 2012, the same week he turned sixty-six years old, leaving behind two great kids and a ton of friends. Not a day goes by that I don't miss him.

While we were growing up, Mike was kind of my spirit guide in the ways of the underground, including mind-altering substances. My first attempts at drug use were disastrous, starting with chugging Romilar cough syrup as a kid, a horrible experience; you could just feel the brain cells melting away. That was followed by smoking banana peels and paregoric-dipped cigarettes—yes, children, we really did try smoking anything and everything back then—and neither did a thing for me.

But then Mike came home from Oberlin bearing marijuana and psychedelics, and suddenly Valhalla was at hand. First time I smoked pot was with Mike over at a friend's house. First I felt light as air, then I could not stop laughing. It was wonderful, mind-blowing and hangover-free, even though some pretty major munchies kicked in. I remember us playing catch with eggs and making quite a mess.

Also mind-blowing were the music and philosophy Mike turned me on to, like giving me Nietzsche to read and playing Charlie Parker and the Lovin' Spoonful when I was fourteen. I felt my vistas expanding in all directions, especially when Mike let me tag along to shows; it helped that I could pass for older, which made Mike and his friends more willing. I got to see some unbelievably cool shit with them, like John Coltrane, king of the bebop saxophonists.

Coltrane's live show was as wild as anything I'd ever heard—skronk of the gods, very different from *Ballads*, *Coltrane's Sound*, and the other records I'd heard. Putting a memorable capper on the whole thing, Coltrane and I briefly met and shook hands that night. To this day, I still meet sax players who want to touch my hand because of that.

I didn't see Stevie Wonder onstage back then, but I did happen to be at 8th Street Music Center in Philly one day in 1966 when he came in to try out the new Maestro phase shifter with his chromatic harmonica, and I got to watch and listen. Amazing. Can't imagine his show that night could have been any better.

I also saw Cream when they came through town, and Janis Joplin with Big Brother & the Holding Company. Janis was one of the best I ever heard, but after the show her rental car wouldn't start in the late-night cold and she didn't know what to do. Fortunately, I knew just enough about cars to make myself useful.

"Looks like this has one of those new automatic chokes," I told her. So I had her driver pop the hood, and I took off the air filter and hit the choke. It started right up, and I closed the hood.

"Thanks, hon," she said, and off they drove, my brush with greatness complete.

Another close encounter was with Grateful Dead guitarist Jerry Garcia, back when the original keyboardist Pigpen was still in the band. After the show I met Garcia, Captain Trips himself, and I bummed a cigarette. Garcia looked me up and down, and damn if he didn't give me the whole pack.

"You look like ya need 'em," he said, and I felt like Elvis himself had just given me a scarf.

So I smoked every last one with relish, and then I hung the empty pack on one of my Little League baseball trophies. It was a fitting symbol of the end of childish ways and days.

# Bright Lights, Big Cities

FOR A LOT OF FOLKS out in cool hippie-paradise places like San Francisco, 1967 was "the Summer of Love." For me, that year was turning sixteen and getting an actual driver's license. No more Vespa for me! Now even when my brother and his friends weren't around, I could get out to some of Philadelphia's finer, freakier live-music establishments on my own. There was the Trauma, a psychedelic joint that lasted long enough for me to see Moby Grape, Lothar and the Hand People, Canned Heat, and other bands flying their freak flag on the circuit back then. After the Trauma closed, a bigger place called the Electric Factory opened and it was more of the same.

At the Electric Factory, I met a fellow named Vince McGarry, who ran the record store and head shop there. Years later, after becoming a recording engineer, Vince would move to Texas, work on a few Asleep at the Wheel records, and marry my ex-girlfriend, proving only what a small world it is. But back then, Vince was also a jazz deejay on WHAT-FM, spinning Coltrane and Miles Davis. Over on WMMR-FM, one of America's earliest underground stations, you'd hear the Doors, Lovin' Spoonful, Rolling Stones, Jefferson Airplane. Then came *Sgt. Pepper's Lonely Hearts Club Band* in June, and everybody's mind was blown all over again. It seemed like all you heard that summer of 1967 was the *Sgt. Pepper's* album or Bobbie Gentry's "Ode to Billie Joe."

Back on the school side of things, I did my last two years of high school at William Penn Charter School for Boys, a blue-blood Quaker prep school with a tie-and-blazer dress code. Originally chartered in 1689, it was very fancy and expensive, and I don't know how I got in or how my parents afforded it. But my mom did some tutoring there, so they must have cut us a break. I don't think it hurt that I was a good basketball player and really tall (even though I was still growing and wouldn't reach my full six-foot-seven-inch height until my early twenties).

Everything was cool with the basketball team until right before my senior year, when the coach delivered an ultimatum: "Get a haircut, or don't show up next year." So I quit. I loved the game but not the coaches, and I was not cutting my hair for nobody.

Besides which, nobody I was playing music with gave a rat's ass about my long hair. Music was still A1 on my jukebox, and the Sixties being the Sixties, drugs were a big part of the experience. Still are. I smoked weed, of course, lots and lots of weed (and I still do). I took acid and psilocybin mushrooms, too, every chance I had, and not just for the hell of it. I was on a quest for knowledge, of myself and the world at large, tuned in to the times—and the times were heavy.

With Vietnam and clashes between generations, sexes, and races, there was war raging at home and abroad. The Sixties decade was when everybody started looking at some of the imperfections beneath the surface of the seemingly innocent *Ozzie and Harriet* middle-class world we'd grown up in, like all that Jim Crow bullshit I'd seen in the South. There was a very real sense of America coming apart at the seams, and it was a scary time that drove families apart.

My dad and I went through a two-year stretch where we did not talk at all, after I started smoking dope and got heavily into the antiwar movement. He saw the folly of the Vietnam War, but he also thought that getting high, marching in the street, and getting arrested over it was stupid.

As far as the drugs went, what I couldn't explain to my dad was that they were a form of therapy, and I think they were actually good for me. They helped me become a freethinker while also sort of steeling me for a lot of what would follow. Hell, if I could survive the psychological demons of an acid trip, the rest of life seemed like a breeze.

In 1969, I turned eighteen and graduated from Penn Charter—technically. They more or less kicked me out of school at the end of the year for misbehavior and general disrespect to authority. But my friend Will Carr (who later put his powers of persuasion to good use by becoming a respected U.S. attorney) convinced them to mail me my diploma if I passed my finals. I didn't want to attend graduation ceremonies anyway, so that was just fine. I passed, and all was well.

A month after that, I went off to Antioch College in Yellow Springs, Ohio. At that time, I wasn't thinking of music as anything like a "career" or a job where you could make a living. So I enrolled at Antioch with the intention of becoming a filmmaker, which seemed like the next best thing. I loved telling stories, and in high school I'd learned how to run the moviola, change film, and do simple technical things like light-meter readings.

Antioch seemed like the place to go for someone like me, because it offered lots of alternative courses and disciplines. It also had a five-year work-study program where you'd alternate between taking classes and doing three-month "co-op job" internships in your chosen field. There were a lot of Antioch alumni in the film business, so the internship gigs and the teachers were cool. One of those teachers was Rod Serling, founder of *The Twilight Zone* TV series, who taught writing for radio and television. But wouldn't you know it, Rod left before I got there.

Still, it worked out okay. I spent that first summer quarter taking classes, doing a little acting in campus productions, and causing trouble. Reading French surrealists like Rimbaud had a profound effect on me, and I'd expound on surrealism as related to Shakespeare's *Richard II* and how great art required suffering. It was horseshit, of course, and not just because I never actually read *Richard II* beyond the Cliff's Notes study-guide version. But I could orate, and in class one day I read a paper aloud that actually made a girl cry. Not a reaction I was used to, but all right.

"Ray borders on genius," the teacher wrote on my paper, "but I would hate to live in his world." That was okay; there wasn't room for him in my world anyway.

I also spent one weekend that August making the scene at a happening you may have heard about, a groovy little gathering called Woodstock. Headed up to Yasgur's Farm in upstate New York with a girl named Judy to get in on the "3 days of Peace & Music," and we wound up having to walk for eight hours because all the highways were at a standstill. Still, it was the most amazing experience. All the people were beautiful, and so friendly, almost like hippie flight attendants: "You want some pot? Something to eat? Anything?"

We finally got to the site, and it was raining so hard there was no music going on. So Judy and I were sitting there getting drenched, wondering what to do, when I saw a friend of mine named Richard Feldman.

"Richard! Baby! What's going on?"

He said it was all fucked up, and we should go down to New York City and hang out there instead. So that's what we did. Left Woodstock without hearing a note but still had a great time. As for Richard, he later went on to be very successful, working with everybody from Eric Clapton to Toots and the Maytals. His timing always was perfect.

After finishing summer classes, I wound up in New York City in the fall of 1969 on one of Antioch's aforementioned cool internships, working on a project with filmmaker Ely Landau. It was called *King: A Filmed Record . . . Montgomery to Memphis*, a four-hour documentary about the late great Martin Luther King Jr. Had all the footage from the Montgomery bus strike to King's assassination in Memphis, with actors like James Earl Jones, Marlon Brando, Sidney Poitier, and Paul Newman reading his speeches.

The director and editor were both Antioch alumni, so that was the hookup. I was an apprentice editor, and I learned the whole editing gig that fall: how to mark film with a grease pencil and cut, splice, do fades, dubs. It's basically the same thing my younger son, Aaron, does now when he cuts movie trailers out in Hollywood, except nowadays it's all done on computer. Back in 1969, we were using razor blades and tape.

I made eighty bucks a week and paid eighty bucks a month in rent, so the bottom line worked out. I lived in an eight-by-ten-foot room in a filthy apartment on St. Mark's Place in the East Village, right across the street from the Electric Circus and around the corner from Fillmore East, which meant I didn't get much sleep. Seeing Santana open for Paul Butterfield just a couple of months after they'd both played Woodstock was probably that fall's musical highlight. I also met Kenneth Anger, the underground filmmaker who was using eight-millimeter cameras and Magic Markers to do these movies that were just bonkers. Morning, noon, and night, it was quite the bustling scene, and I got the complete New York City experience.

Workdays, I'd wake up early, put on a coat and tie, and ride the subway to work while watching the most beautiful women on earth, wondering how I could talk to them. But nobody talks to anybody in New York unless they're crazy, in which case they're probably talking to themselves. So I kept to myself. When I wasn't doing the hands-on editing, I'd fetch coffee and pastries (a chore I hated), answer phones, and do whatever else needed doing.

It was fun being on my own in New York as a rambunctious teenager, and the filmmaking knowledge I picked up has come in handy over the years. But it did not take long for me to realize that I was no filmmaker, mostly because of my attention deficit disorder. I just couldn't see spending ten years to get a single film done—and that's if I was lucky. I'd much rather just go down to the Village, find an open-mike night somewhere, and play a song I'd written the night before. A timeline like that was a lot more my speed.

I also realized that even though I loved New York, big-city life there or in Los Angeles just was not for me. And while I was at it, school wasn't for me, either. It was time to chuck everything and take a new course.

With a plan germinating, I began plotting my getaway.

At one time during high school, I'd had a clear path to being a doctor if I'd only wanted to follow it. Jefferson Medical College in Philadelphia had a program for gifted science students, and I was accepted, even though I don't know how "gifted" I was. Still, the people in charge saw something in me, and I could have stuck with that. But the more I saw of the medical profession, the less I agreed with the hierarchical way it was done in this country.

I couldn't abide medicine or filmmaking, thanks to my ADD. Music, however, was still just as strong a passion as ever. Even during my aspiring-filmmaker period in New York, I played every chance I could with Peter Brown, a friend I'd known since elementary school.

Out of all the music I was playing and listening to, what spoke to me the most was old country music—people like Ernest Tubb and Bob Wills, artists who were out of fashion in every way. Even Nashville wasn't interested in Ernest Tubb anymore because he represented the old hillbilly ways that seemed to embarrass the country establishment—or as they put it, he "sang out of tune." Uh-huh, right.

Admittedly, country music seemed like a weird place for someone like me to want to find a home from a cultural standpoint. Topping the country charts in the fall of 1969 was "Okie from Muskogee" by Merle Haggard, a musical icon who would later become a very dear friend, collaborator, and fellow traveler. But back then, his singing "Okie" seemed like a call to arms against . . . well, me and every other long-haired dope fiend out there.

Somehow, none of that even fazed me. Most of the antiwar types I knew were into jazz, and we'd all get together, get high, and play weird avant-garde jazz. I'd try to sneak a country song in there now and then, which made them laugh. But even my jazz-snob friends had to admit that country music was genuinely "of the people," which only made me more determined. Strip away the political associations of its time, and country was the most purely American music we had.

The more I talked it over with friends, the more a conviction took hold: I was going to form a working-class country band and be accepted, even though I was not one of those people. I considered it a grand and noble social experiment. If a Jewish Yankee like me could play this music I loved and find acceptance among the working class, it would be a shining example of brotherhood for all. My ambition was to be a Renaissance man, master of many pursuits: guitarist, singer, songwriter, bandleader, businessman, artist, philanthropist, community leader, and wandering minstrel, all rolled into one.

I wanted to bring this great music back and win over a new generation of kids by presenting it in unexpected ways—to take the wide-open spaces of Western swing and decorate them with flourishes of Count Basie–style big-band jazz, say. Or create something like Buck Owens's Buckaroos with Charlie Parker sitting in on saxophone. Or as I put it in my journal at the time, I was going to "complete the circle, bring the roots of country music back to the generation whose parents loved the music, but in the upheaval of the '60s lost its soul to the plastic white-bread culture that drove the kids away from the music."

In short, my goal was nothing less than to rediscover America through music—and to have a blast doing it, of course. That was the ride. The only thing I didn't have yet was a band of like-minded misfits to take it with me.

# Almost Heaven, West Virginia

THE WHEELS WERE turning and change was in the air in late 1969 when I went back to Antioch, where I moved with three friends into an apartment so small I didn't even get half of a room to share. My space was a mattress on the living-room floor. But that was fine because I wasn't there much. Too busy elsewhere.

That was around the time I met Ed Ward, later a writer of much renown for *Rolling Stone* magazine. But back then, Ed was another Antioch student who also taught a class on rock 'n' roll. Being the resident audiovisual guy, I would run tape machines and such for the music department. So Ed and I got to be friends from me helping run the technical side of his classes.

Ed was on Antioch's concert committee, too, and one day he tipped me off about a show he'd just booked. It was a band from California with a freaky name, Commander Cody and His Lost Planet Airmen. They hadn't put out an album yet, and they were still a few years away from their big hit "Hot Rod Lincoln" (which would crack the Top 10 of the charts in 1972). At that point, they were spending most of their time touring as a support act for the Byrds, Amboy Dukes, and other big acts of the day, and playing clubs on their own. The main reason I went to their show at the Antioch Student Center was that I was friends with everybody in the opening act, a student group called Ed Chicken and the

French Fries. And my pals were good, but God almighty, Cody was a revelation that blew my head wide open. It was, as they say, the start of a beautiful friendship.

Cody's real name was George Frayne and he played barrelhouse piano while leading the loudest, wildest band I'd ever heard. They played a crazed, amped-up countrified rockabilly that swung hard and rocked even harder, and the way they combined it all was everything I envisioned music could be. Whatever style of music you liked was probably somewhere in the DNA of what Cody was playing—how could anybody not like these guys? Impossible.

It was obvious to me that this was the mother lode I'd been searching for: a country-western rockabilly band doing some swing, and rocking hard enough to take on all comers. Cody and the band had cracked the code, and all I could do was stare in awestruck wonder. I went up to their bespectacled guitar player afterward, the great Bill Kirchen, and all but bowed down before him. How in the hell did they do that? I wanted to know.

All these years later, Cody and Kirchen are still some of my best friends out there, stand-up guys and fellow travelers on the roots-music circuit. When I started my own musical journey not long after that first encounter, they would be among the first to lend a helping hand, which is something I'll never forget. But the best thing they did for me was to show the way forward and suggest how to present everything I was hearing in my head in a unified, rockin', rollin', boogie-down package.

I had the statement-of-purpose manifesto, and I'd seen a model of how it could work on a stage. Now I just needed co-conspirators to bring it to life.

My old childhood pal Reuben Gosfield was also enrolled at Antioch, but at a different campus. He was 450 miles away from Yellow Springs at Antioch's campus in Columbia, Maryland. But he and I were still thick as thieves, constantly in touch and plotting. Also entering our circle around then was Gene Preston, a native of Vermont who shared an apartment with my sister,

Sandy, and her husband, Gerry, at Northeastern University. We'd get together to jam and talk endlessly about music, life, culture, the future.

We were of like mind about the importance of music and how we wanted to bring back real country music. To do that, we decided what we had to do was get back to the country: drop out of school and go someplace remote to hole up and start a band.

First, however, we had to run the gauntlet of getting through the damn draft lottery. Even though the Vietnam War had peaked in 1968, it was still raging full-on as 1969 turned into 1970. Uncle Sam was still in a terrible jam and in need of draftee manpower, and I'm sure we were tempting specimens for conscription. Quitting school meant giving up our student deferments and leaving ourselves open to getting drafted—a risky thing to do.

But it all depended on where your number landed in the lottery. The way it worked is you were assigned a number based on your birthday. Anything under 100 meant you'd almost certainly be selected by your friends and neighbors to serve, which meant getting drafted and sent off to battle the red menace. Over 100, you had a shot at getting out of it. And if you were over 200, you were all set, no sweat.

We were sweating plenty and praying for high numbers when word came back from the draft board. And hallelujah, the word was good. Reuben and I drew 256 and 258, and Gene was somewhere in the same vicinity. So we were all home free. We wouldn't have to go into the military, or follow Jesse Winchester's lead and run away to Canada.

But I was planning on running away someplace, all right, and I wasn't going alone. I've always been a good salesman—skilled at peddling ice to Eskimos, as they say. But this was a harder sell: "Come with me to middle-of-nowhere Bumfuck to start a country band. We've got no money, jobs, prospects, or even electricity or food, and we'll be playing music that's sure to confuse *everybody*. So whattaya say?" Somehow I talked a few people into it. Don't ask me how.

By the end of 1969, we had a destination picked out for our adventure: an outback tract near Paw Paw, a town of 706 souls in the wilderness of deepest West Virginia. It was in the middle of nowhere, but owned by a friend's family. As Antioch's winter term wound down and on-campus conversations turned to plans for the spring, I started telling friends the news: "Me and Reuben and another guy named Gene Preston are all gonna move to a farm outside of Paw Paw, West Virginia, and start up a country-western band." To a person, everybody looked at me like I'd lost my mind. Two of us were Jewish and all three of us were longhairs, going into the redneck wilds of West Virginia to start up an old-time country band. What could possibly go wrong? Cue "Dueling Banjos."

I couldn't wait.

My parents, however, were decidedly less than thrilled, especially my dad. When I told him I was quitting school, he flipped his lid and thundered about how I better not expect any more money out of him. I told him I didn't want any of his money. Ah, youth.

So, anyway, that was the end of my formal schooling. All these years later, the only paper I've got is a high school diploma—everything else has been postgraduate work in the school of hard knocks. I still have people coming to me all the time, asking what to do if your kid wants to be a musician. I tell parents to be as encouraging and supportive as they can while drilling into their kids that they've got to either have a Plan B or accept that they'll never make much money. A career in music is a vow of poverty for most people, so you've got to love it.

When I hit the road to commence my own musical adventure in March of 1970, I was part of a wave of friends coming from Antioch. I traveled with Ben Schneeberg in his Volkswagen Microbus. Coming a bit later were Eddy Freeman and Truffy Angleton, both of Ed Chicken and the French Fries (Truffy was also the son of James Angleton, who was then head of counterintelligence at the CIA).

We left Yellow Springs on eastbound Interstate 70 and drove all night through Ohio to Wheeling, West Virginia, just short of the Pennsylvania state line. Then we picked up Old Highway 40 and took that down through Maryland's western panhandle. Acutely aware of the righteousness of our quest and cause, we set the mood by listening to AM country radio the whole way. "Okie from Muskogee" was still in power rotation on every country station in America—a reminder that whether in glory or folly, we were bound for the hippie equivalent of Injun country. Like Lewis and Clark before us, we were going off the map.

Crossing into West Virginia, we came to Berkeley Springs, where George Washington had gone to soothe his war wounds after becoming the first U.S. president nearly two centuries earlier. Then we took Route 9 through Capon Bridge and Largent before arriving in the small town of Paw Paw, the last stop before crossing the Potomac River back into Maryland. Reuben had driven his 1965 Plymouth Belvedere out from Columbia and met us at our destination, a farm in the country near Paw Paw and the even smaller crossroads hamlet of Neals Run. When Ben and I got there, the gate was locked, so we had to park just outside it and hike in through the snow. It was about a mile but felt longer (especially with Ben asking every five minutes, "You sure this is the right place?").

Traveling to West Virginia felt like going back in time to the Great Depression because it was a desperately poor part of the world—lots of unemployment, food stamps, welfare, and moonshine. But that farm felt like going back even further, all the way to the Colonial era. The oldest part of the farmhouse dated to the late 1700s and was a cabin made of hand-hewn logs two feet square. It was surrounded by orchards that had been actively producing apple and peach harvests as recently as the 1950s, but had hardly been touched since.

There was almost no evidence of recent human habitation anywhere on that spread, except for one thing: a working jeep, an old Army surplus model like what you'd see in a World War II movie. We started it up and it ran great, but you want your vehicles to stop as well as go and we soon discovered that jeep had no brakes. Only way to stop it was to put it in first gear and four-wheel drive, shut down the motor, and let it buck to a stop. We quickly got used to the jeep's funky ways, but it scared plenty of other folks. Not long after our arrival, the 1970 census takers were passing through Paw Paw, and we drove into town to be counted—and almost gave the poor census taker lady a heart attack because she was sure we weren't going to stop before running her down. Sorry about that, ma'am.

Nevertheless, the census made it official: we were, God help us, residents of West Virginia (where we boosted the population of Neals Run by three). Mountaineers are always free.

# *A Name of Our Own*

ONCE WE GOT to the farmhouse and unpacked, we went to survey our new surroundings. There was a swing on the front porch, so that was good, and we were glad to have a structure for shelter. But on the downside, the place had no electricity, plumbing, or other modern conveniences, so it was just short of camping in the wilderness. The provisions we'd brought along weren't going to last forever, at which point we'd have to start foraging. Become hunter-gatherer scavengers—or cannibals.

First things first, however. We had a honky-tonk band to start!

We actually had some decent gear, courtesy of the great bluesman Taj Mahal. He had played at Antioch's Student Center the previous term and left behind a darned fine PA system, which went unclaimed. So I inherited it after school let out. And our power problem was solved when Eddy went up to his mother's house in Bucks County, Pennsylvania, and liberated a gas-powered generator. He brought it back, we fired it up, and went electric, just like Dylan in '65.

The cold-storage building by the orchard had the most room, so we tried to use that for a rehearsal space. But it was kind of an acoustic disaster. Even after we stacked apple crates to create walls and form a makeshift room in the center, it never improved beyond an echo-plagued mess. So we gave up on that and set up shop inside the packinghouse next to the cabin; also not perfect, but it had plenty of room and worked well enough for our purposes.

Gene made it down from Boston, and we commenced to fiddling around. We had us a fluid cast of characters in Paw Paw, a lot of people always coming and going, but the band's constants would be Reuben, Gene, and me. We switched around between instruments a good bit. I'd mostly play guitar or bass while Reuben and Gene switched between guitar and drums, and we all kind of sang; none of us were exactly confident vocalists at that point except for Truffy, who did a mean "Party Lights." Eddy would join in on electric Wurlitzer piano. Reuben's friend Larry, whose father owned the Paw Paw farm, didn't play anything, but he was around to lend moral support.

Eventually, we were also joined by another friend from Washington, D.C., Hal Ganz, who became our bass player. The lineup stabilized with Gene on drums, me on guitar, and Reuben on steel guitar.

We started out just playing songs everybody already knew by the likes of Ernest Tubb, Buck Owens, and, of course, Hank Williams. George Jones's "The Race Is On" was an early favorite, and we'd throw in the occasional non-country wild card, too, Fats Domino or Buddy Holly. We'd also take folk songs, Beatles tunes, or *Smokey Joe's Café* and do 'em up as country. Occasionally, we'd even try to write songs of our own, some of them even decent.

Not too long into our existence, we played our first performance for somebody other than each other, a "show" for an audience of one. It was a fellow named Bill Miller, who lived in Paw Paw but had a small hunter's cabin on some land he owned up above our farm. He would pass through on the way to his cabin, and we'd chat. One time he stopped by in the middle of practice, and we invited him to stay and listen. He told us we sounded real good and even though I'm sure he was just being polite, it was still nice to hear.

After he'd hung out with us enough to decide we were all right, Bill became a valuable friend. He ran interference for us with the locals, telling everyone that we were just "good ol' hippies" who weren't to be feared, and not like the animal-sacrificing, Satan-worshipping freaks they'd heard about.

With Bill as our envoy, we were ambassadors of understanding between rednecks and longhairs. Can't we all just get along? Yes, we can.

We hadn't been at it for very long when we decided we should all adopt stage names. Between Seifert and Gosfield, our real names just weren't colorful enough to pass muster on the honky-tonk circuit. So Reuben became Lucky Oceans; just a name he made up, trying to come up with an old bluesman's name that had kind of a hippie vibe. Gene wasn't Jewish, but his full name was the all-too-plain Eugene Leroy Preston. So he dropped his first name to become Leroy Preston, a name that sounded like either a ranch hand or a Dallas Cowboys running back. But it worked.

Me, I went the opposite direction from Lucky and Leroy because it wasn't my first name that was the problem. I'd read about how Ray Charles Robinson dropped his last name to adopt the performing name Ray Charles, so that no one would confuse him with the boxer Sugar Ray Robinson. If it was good enough for Ray Robinson, it was good enough for Ray Seifert. I dropped Seifert and became "Professionally Known As" Ray Benson, keeping Ray Seifert as my legal name. Over the years, that's been handy. If a call comes in for Ray Seifert, then we know it's a credit-card company, stockbroker, or someone else I don't want to talk to.

Ray Benson is a character I made up, bigger than Ray Seifert all the way around. I was conflicted about that at first because in 1970, everybody was all hung up on that Age of Aquarius notion of "authenticity" and one's "true self." But don't we all take on roles? Wear the clothes we want to wear, talk the way we want to talk?

Consider my friend Tony Visconti, an Italian kid from New York who went off to England and reinvented himself as the quintessential British studio guy. Tony thrived over there, producing David Bowie and T. Rex; later he married John Lennon's old girlfriend May Pang and even developed an English accent, the better to fit in as a member of British rock royalty.

Me, I wanted to become a country singer even though I'd grown up Jewish in Philadelphia. But that wasn't going to stop me any more than it stopped Hank Snow, who was born in Nova Scotia and still made the Country Music Hall of Fame. In dressing and acting the part of country singer, I eventually became one.

Of course, our band still needed a name, and there should be a long and complicated story about how we chose Asleep at the Wheel. But the simple truth is that Lucky came up with it while sitting in the Paw Paw farm's old fiberglass outhouse. He was in there tending to business one day, when a vision came to him and he burst out. He may have even still had his pants down.

"Hey!" he yelled. "I've got it! Our name! From now on, we're Asleep at the Wheel."

We kicked that around and had a bit of discussion, but really not that much. The name stuck, and from that day to this, we've always been Asleep at the Wheel. The name used to puzzle people and make them wonder if we were a cult, but either you got it or you didn't. If you got it, no explanation was necessary and if you didn't, none would suffice. I even worked up a little stage routine about it to introduce us to crowds at shows:

> Imagine yourself in your car or in your truck, drivin' late at night on a loooooong lonesome highway. Many many miles you've been traveling, and many many more miles you got to go. But as the night progresses, you begin to get tired. And as your car hurtles along the highway, you lose consciousness and right then and there . . . you know just how we feel . . .
>
> . . . 'CAUSE ALL OF US TONIGHT, WE ARE ASLEEP AT THE WHEEL!

Yep, that's us. Forty years later, I went back to Paw Paw and visited the farm where it all began. And I couldn't believe it, but somehow the outhouse where Lucky thought of the name was still standing.

As the band continued to woodshed, we also learned how to survive in our rural surroundings. Music, after all, was only one part of our back-to-nature adventure. The other part of the mission was learning to live in harmony with nature. So we embraced sustainable, eco-friendly organic farming and alternative energy—alternative as in manual labor, because we had no choice. We didn't have much in the way of tools and machines, or money to buy any, so we had to do a lot by hand.

Admittedly, there were times when the whole one-with-nature part of the trip was a bit much. Lucky us, our arrival coincided with the once-every-seventeen-years cycle of locusts, and we had to contend with a damn-near-Bible-sized plague of the noisy bastards. We'd brought along a female cat named Li'l Fucker, and she had a litter of cute little black kittens. They had a great time hunting locusts all day and all night, but it would have taken an army of cats to contain them.

Meantime, we learned to live off the bounty of the land, which wasn't hard because things grew freely there. We'd collect berries, wild greens, wild chamomile, mint, and sassafras. We baked bread in the farmhouse's wood-burning stove, and we did a little hunting—rabbit, squirrel, fish, and one deer. None of us had a license for any of it, of course (including a couple of local friends, Denny and DeLyle, who would bring us deer they killed), but it was either hunt to subsist or starve. After killing a deer, we butchered and cured the meat into jerky, hamburger, and venison. Lucky even tanned the hide to make a rug that was very, very stiff. It still felt like an accomplishment.

When the band wasn't playing, we'd hike around and explore the countryside. All of us got pretty skilled at using an axe, which was good because there was always wood to chop. Somebody brought along a copy of the famous outdoorsman Euell

Gibbons's back-to-nature book *Stalking the Wild Asparagus*, which was handy. The locals taught us how to collect and cook poke salad, which was handier.

We had an idyllic stretch of months on the Paw Paw farm as spring stretched into summer, before our reverie was rudely interrupted. Lucky's friend Larry was our hookup for that place, and he'd assured us it was cool for us to adopt it as our residence. But it seems he'd never actually gotten permission for us to be there. So when Larry's dad showed up unannounced, he demanded to know, "Who the hell are you and what are you doing on my property?!" We had two weeks to clear out.

That was a setback, but Lucky put the time to good use and found us another place not too many miles away near a town called Levels, West Virginia. Population about three dozen, Levels consisted of ten or twelve houses and one general store. The house Lucky found us was about two miles out of town, down a dirt road with a steep drop-off into a hundred-foot gorge on the side. Getting there was harrowing.

Once we did, it was a grand house and much plusher than what we'd had in Paw Paw—a late-1800s-vintage mansion with hardwood floors and a big wide staircase suitable for descending in a hoop skirt. We fixed that place up pretty nice: soundproofed a practice room, built an outhouse and even a sauna. Along with raising chickens for the eggs and goats for the milk (shades of unpasteurized European milk, drinkable but kinda gross), we started a garden with sweet corn, squash, tomatoes, green beans, spinach, carrots, and beets. We had just enough time to lay in food before winter came on.

# Asleep at the Wheel Goes to Washington

ONE AFTERNOON during our time at the Paw Paw house, a couple of thirty-foot school buses pulled up and opened their doors, and out spilled a bunch of hippies. That was our introduction to "the Hog Farm," a traveling entertainment-activist commune that had formed the year before at Woodstock. The ringleader was Wavy Gravy, Woodstock's self-appointed "Chief of the Please Force" and all-around bon vivant of America's underground railroad. He dressed up like a clown because, he said, it made him less likely to get arrested. When the movie about his life came out, it was called *Saint Misbehavin'*. Yep, one of ours, for sure. Anyway, Wavy and his mob showed up on our doorstep, and it was a scene straight out of Dr. Livingstone, I presume.

"We were getting gas at this little place," they told us, "and the guy said there was a hippie band that lived not far from here. So we got directions, and here we are."

Of course, we took them in for a spell. The locals in West Virginia were fun to hang out with, but there was still something to be said for time spent with fellow travelers who spoke the same language we did. We talked of life, love, music, living off the land, self-sufficiency, farming—and mind-altering substances, of course. Just across the river, we'd heard, there was a hemp field that had been there since World War II. So we mounted an excursion with some of our Hog Farmer visitors and waded on over. Sure enough, we found several acres of six-foot-high hemp plants swaying in the breeze. The farmer who owned it chased us off, but not before we got away with half a dozen plants.

It turned out the Hog Farmers were on their way to Washington, D.C., about three hours away, and they invited us to come along after hearing us play. There was even a gig in it for us. A free show, so no money; but sharing a bill with Alice Cooper and Jefferson Airplane's blues-band spin-off, Hot Tuna—not bad, given that we'd still never played for more than an audience of one. So we said yes and it was a blast, our first show ever. My brother Mike was even part of it.

Still, that was kind of a rough day for me. Chronic back problems are a major downside of being as tall as I am, and I've always had issues. First time my back went out, I was sixteen years old and they gave me a muscle relaxant called Parafon Forte—chlorzoxazone, a little speed and a little downer, and it fucked me up but good. Last time I ever took that.

Well, just my luck that my back started acting up again the day of our D.C. debut. Paul from the Hog Farm crew took pity on me and passed along some peyote. A hallucinogenic substance may not have been the most direct way to deal with pain, but it worked a hell of a lot better than Parafon Forte—definitely took my mind off my back and made for a most interesting set. We did our usual funky country-western truck-driving music, and it went over like dynamite with the big-city freaks.

Capping a truly surreal day, a reporter came up afterward and conducted an interview with a very stoned yours truly. My first-ever interview, thank ya very much, and I can't imagine I made too much sense in my addled state. But that didn't keep me from having plenty to say about the state of the nation and how we wanted to tear down the walls dividing us all.

It was the end of the 1960s, but the start of something else. Asleep at the Wheel was becoming one of the few proud and brave bands that could play for hippies and hicks alike, entertain both audiences, and explain it all to the media afterward in good sound-bite form. Hawks-and-doves hostility over the Vietnam War was still incredibly intense, and the generation gap seemed wider than ever. And yet there we were, a band of young longhairs smoking our smoke, playing our country songs, and feelin' groovy.

It felt like we were exactly where we needed to be.

As longhairs out in the country, we stood out as objects of fascination to the local redneck populace in West Virginia. They were always coming around to gawk, which could have been awkward. But, ever mindful of our mission of brotherhood, we always went out of our way to be welcoming to all. Mostly, it worked out, like the time a little old guy named Ceder Amica showed up. Ceder looked to be about sixty-five years old, and he was maybe five-foot-four. We got to talking and he told us about his nephew John Amica, a truck driver who also ran a joint outside Paw Paw called the Sportsman's Club. Maybe we'd like to play there?

John himself came by and offered us a regular Sunday-night gig. No cover charge or guarantee, just pass the hat. But we weren't exactly in a position to be picky. So we took it, moving from playing in one house to another—a cinder-block addition bankrolled by John's mother, Margaret. Real plush, high-dollar place, the Sportsman's Club.

About fifty people showed up the first time Asleep at the Wheel played the Sportsman's Club, and we did our usual assortment of covers—Hank, Merle, Ernest, Buck, Moon Mullican, Johnny Cash. You can't go wrong with Johnny Cash songs, especially if you're a baritone like me. We also dusted off "Wabash Cannonball" and Woody Guthrie's "Do Re Mi," and I guess those folks liked us pretty well. Our take at the end of the night was $50; John himself kicked in $15 of that because he'd done well enough at the bar to be feeling generous.

There was, however, at least one guy in the house who did not dig us one little bit. During the break, a fellow calling himself "Oklahoma Red Rider" came around and announced that after our next set, he'd be coming back to "kick all your hippie asses."

Well, now, that didn't sound too friendly. But on we played.

By the end of the next set, everybody had had plenty to drink, including our new friend from the Sooner State. As promised, Red returned, but we talked him into settling it by arm-wrestling our bass player, Hal—who, appearances aside, was well versed in isometric training and pretty much unbeatable as a champion arm wrestler. Not knowing what he was in for, Red agreed to the match, they went at it, and Hal beat him easily. We all hooted. How about *that*? But Red, to his credit, was a good sport about the whole thing.

"We're all gonna drink this till it's empty," he declared, holding up a bottle, and we did. No pain. No gain, either, but at least there was no pain. And so a potential beating disaster turned into yet another cultural exchange along the redneck-hippie divide, which looked to be shrinking all the time in our world.

We went back to the Sportsman's Club the next Sunday and did even better, making $75. Already, things were going in the right direction.

As 1971 came on, we kept playing for the hillbilly crowds at the Sportsman's Club in Paw Paw and also going into D.C. to play for big-city crowds whenever we got a chance, at clubs like the Emergency. Our most regular D.C. club was called Tammany Hall, a joint five blocks from the White House with a crowd you'd call "eclectic" in the *Casablanca* sense of the term. Little bar, held maybe fifty people. Billy O'Brien was the manager and bartender, and his idea of a bar was to cater to a cast of characters regularly watering there and giving the place atmosphere. We were part of the vibe, too, and we got a nice little following there.

Never did see President Nixon at Tammany, but there were lots of his henchmen around, plus other politicos, the occasional visiting celebrity—and Peter Sheridan, one of the legendary crazy people of the entertainment industry, who would be in and out of our lives repeatedly over the next decade. Peter was a big, brawling guy, a few years older than us, whose idea of a prank was to put LSD on the doorknobs of the police station.

Since he was a member of the pro-acid Neo-American Church (a group that believed mankind's ultimate purpose was to destroy the planet Saturn), I guess that was an outreach tactic.

Peter wound up in California hanging around the Grateful Dead for a few years before he moved to Texas in the mid-'70s and fell in with Willie Nelson's entourage. He'd do things like trade Willie's car for some pot, or visit Willie's beleaguered booking agent (Jim Wyatt, who was later head of William Morris) by riding his BSA chopper up the steps and into the building. Eventually, Peter died on that motorcycle in a 1980 traffic accident, God rest his soul. A biker to the end.

I was a biker myself off and on for years, and I've always collected motorcycles and instruments—best investments I've ever made and I never lost a dime at either. I'll buy guitars and keep them until I need the money, although I never seem to sell them and they take up a lot of room. But I play 'em all. As for motorcycles, my most active time in that world was when I lived in the Bay Area in the early '70s. There was no better place to ride motorcycles than California, and I'd ride the hell out of a friend's Lightning Chopper out there.

That put me in contact with a lot of the Hells Angels who'd been at Altamont for the Rolling Stones' 1969 show. I got friendly with one named Deacon Proudfoot, who succeeded Sonny Barger as president. Deacon came to see Asleep at the Wheel play at the Boarding House in San Francisco once, and he offered me a ride back to Oakland. We were going at least a hundred miles an hour over the Bay Bridge when the cops started up with their lights blazing. Deacon didn't stop until he got all the way across; then he pulled over, went back to the cop car, came back and shrugged, "Let's go." I guess they had a deal with the cops.

I finally got a bike of my own in 1976 in Texas, a 1969 Electra Glide for $2,500. I rode that for a year or so until somebody ran a stop sign and I hit him broadside, and the bike stopped. But I didn't, and time stood still as I flew through the air.

I was luckier than Peter Sheridan.

Back at Tammany, we were getting free drinks, free bar food, *and* $125 a night, which felt like living the high life. Not that any of us saved a dime, of course. We were young, broke, and having a ball. So was everybody else we met, like Emmylou Harris—another Tammany regular, still a couple of years away from teaming up with Gram Parsons and truly finding that angelic voice of hers. There was also Fat City, the duo of Bill Danoff and Taffy Nivert, who were the songwriters behind John Denver's "Take Me Home, Country Roads." A few years later, they would hook up with the producer Phil Ramone, become Starland Vocal Band, have a gigantic hit in 1976 with "Afternoon Delight," and win two Grammys. In 1971, however, they were living hand to mouth just as much as we were.

But those were peers we'd bump into. The legends, we'd go out of our way to see. The first chance I got to experience Ernest Tubb, the one and only Texas Troubadour himself, was during Asleep at the Wheel's West Virginia days. He was playing about an hour and a half away at a place in Maryland, and no way was I missing my idol, a singer who was my vocal mentor even if he didn't know it. Two of my favorite singers were Bob Dylan and Ernest Tubb, stylists who sang much like they talked and proved you didn't need a "pretty" voice to make it. Plus Ernest had the greatest band on the road. They wore matching suits with "Texas Troubadour" creased cowboy hats. Too cool.

So we loaded everybody up and went to see Ernest, and let me tell you, it was incredible. I'd never heard a live country band playing jazz—I mean, a real country-western band straight out of a honky-tonk, playing swing like Duke Ellington mixed in with country standards and radio hits of the day. It was like seeing Bob Wills updated from his 1940s heyday to the present—and that was all before the star even appeared onstage.

About forty-five minutes in, a voice intoned, "And now, ladies and gentlemen, the Texas Troubadour . . . *Ernest Tubb*!" And there he was, striding out to "Walking the Floor over You," wearing a white hat and every Western accoutrement you could imagine, playing a Martin guitar with his name inlaid on the neck. The word “Thanks” was on the back, and he’d flash that to the crowd between songs. “Awesome” does not even begin to describe it.

Watching Ernest perform was like seeing the entire history of country music unfold on the stage—part Texas roadhouse, part Grand Ole Opry and all Ernest Tubb. And his jus’-folks way with a crowd made it a master class in showmanship, too. At one point, he looked out from the stage with a twinkle in his eye and said, “This next one goes out to Helen Moreland, who is, oh my, eighty-two years old this week. Happy birthday, darlin’, so good to see ya out and lookin’ so purty.” And out in the audience, Helen Moreland was just swooning. Now that, my friends, is how you maintain a fan base and build the kind of loyalty that sustains a fifty-year career.

Between sets, Lucky and I were in the bathroom and crossed paths with Tubb’s guitarist, Jack Mollette. He looked us up and down.

“Y’all pickers?” he asked.

Yeah, we said, we were, and he nodded.

“Thought so,” he said, smiling. “Y’all don’t look like civilians.”

Asleep at the Wheel started getting a few private-party gigs around D.C. during this period, too, mostly at conventions or embassy functions where a long-haired country band like us was viewed as “colorful.” Sometimes gigs like that could be pretty weird. One night at Tammany, a couple of guys in dark blue suits came in and asked if we’d come over to the Shoreham Hotel nearby after our last set to play at one a.m. for some kind of Southern bankers’ convention. They offered us $75 and a few bottles of booze. Sure, we said, why not?

So the deal was that the blue-suit guys thought it would be a hilarious joke for their straitlaced, churchgoing Southern banker brethren to see hippie freaks like us playing country music in the middle of the night. Hard to predict how such a thing was going to go down, so I fortified myself ahead of time with a couple of marijuana brownies. And everything went just fine until the noise complaints started coming in, at which point the hotel pulled the plug and cut power to the suite where we were playing—right about when the pot brownies were kicking in. That's, uh, really not the best time for lights-out. But we survived.

More than twenty years later, at Bill Clinton's first presidential inauguration in 1993, we would play an event at that same hotel with Willie Nelson. That was a pretty amazing time. We'd known Clinton for years, after meeting him in the mid-'80s playing these parties that Tyson Foods would throw in Arkansas. Small world, especially for those of us on the song-and-dance-and-rubber-chicken circuit.

Meanwhile, things were still booming for Asleep at the Wheel back at the Sportsman's Club in Paw Paw. At a certain point, we got established enough to move from Sunday-night tip-jar freebie to Saturday-night main-draw headliner. We'd charge a $1 cover and pack the place out with an assortment of the local hillbillies, visitors from D.C., and every hippie within a hundred-mile radius. Even though the locals didn't much care for hippies as a breed, we were *their* hippies, by God—and wearing really cool Western clothes, too, so that made it okay. There were nights when we made $150, a lot of dough for that time. Things were good.

But all things must pass, as Beatle George Harrison put it around that time. One day, Lucky and my brother Mike were at a nearby house they thought was abandoned, scavenging for firewood and fixtures for our place in Levels. Turned out it was not an abandoned house after all. The owner appeared, packing heat, and he had them arrested for breaking and entering. At that time, Charles Manson's murder trial was front-page news, so the prospect of bloodthirsty hippie cults running wild in the country was something that put the authorities on edge. Lucky and Mike were looking at actual prison time, until the parents intervened and talked Sergeant Huff into letting them go (good thing, too—a decade or so later, that same jail in Romney, West Virginia, burned down with some prisoners trapped inside).

Mike and Lucky's freedom came at a price for all of us, however. Part of their deal was that they had to leave Hampshire

County, which meant we were on the move again. Lucky found us yet another remote-outback farm, in the nearly abandoned Potomac River town of Magnolia just across the Morgan County line, and we rented it for fifty-five bucks a month. It came with a forty-acre tract of tillable land and was newer than our other West Virginia abodes—built in the early twentieth century, and it actually had electricity. There was no plumbing, but a freshwater spring ran nearby. Compared to our mansion in Levels, the house was much smaller, and it had only two bedrooms. So we turned various sheds and chicken coops on the premises into sleep shacks and carried on as before.

We'd come a long way in a short time, carving out the beginnings of a career. But even after having to move twice, Asleep at the Wheel was still only about eight miles from Paw Paw.

# *Go West, Young Man (and Woman)*

SMALL THOUGH IT WAS, the Magnolia house would be like the "Big Pink" house was for Bob Dylan and the Band, where Asleep at the Wheel really became something unique. Getting from good to great took an endless series of gigs and rehearsals, and some highly impassioned knock-down-drag-out arguments. There might not be universal agreement on this point, but by then I was already pretty much in charge of the band. While it was not exactly 100 percent hard and fast (and by necessity filtered through whatever stimulants were prevailing amongst us at any given moment), Asleep at the Wheel had an agreement that basically went like this:

> If we can't agree on something, Ray will serve as arbitrator and make the final decision.

Whether this was an "agreement" per se or something I bullied my way into is probably in the eye of the beholder. But whatever the details, I took on the role of enlightened despot. And I'm still an enlightened despot, because it turned out to be an arrangement that worked well back then and still does now. My college guidance counselor wasn't good for much, but he did give me a very helpful piece of advice when I was dropping out of school: "Democracies don't work in bands." Amen to that.

I think back to a scene in *The Love of the Last Tycoon*, F. Scott Fitzgerald's great unfinished novel about Irving Thalberg, the boy genius of Hollywood's silent-film era. Thalberg's character is on the first transcontinental airplane flight from New York to L.A., sitting with the head of a railroad company, and they're flying over mountains. "See those mountains?" the railroad guy asks. "We have to put train lines through there. There are countless ways, over this mountain or through that gorge. My job isn't to pick the best route, but to convince everyone that the route we're taking is best." There are many ways to skin a cat, and you've just got to convince the world—or at least your band—that your way is right.

Still, I've always tried not to make my role as Alpha Dog at the Wheel a totally fascist experience. Input has always been free and open, because I can't say that my ideas are always better than anybody else's. Others have certainly had lots of bright-idea moments throughout the band's history, like Lucky coming up with the lightning-bolt inspiration of our name. Then as well as now, I've always relied heavily on those around me because my best talent has always been feeding off talented people and getting them to do their best (and sometimes that involves pushing). But it's always been me articulating Asleep at the Wheel's vision and driving the production end of the band, even when we've worked with outside producers. Leroy always wrote a lot more songs for the band than I did, but I set the production direction by taking everyone's best ideas and making them work. Guess you'd say it was subjective consensus.

Yes, I was an asshole a lot of the time, and I regret a lot of the toes I stepped on, but there were some things I had to do to make it work. It's not like I always had all the answers and everybody else was wrong, but I do think I was the only one who really saw the big picture. That didn't make me any good at diplomacy. Floyd Domino always used to say I had a problem with authority, and I did. That goes two ways; I wasn't too gracious about being challenged, either.

Eldon Shamblin, one of the great guitarists in Bob Wills's Texas Playboys and a hero of mine, once told a mutual friend,

"Tell Ray he's supposed to be having fun!" His philosophy was that nothing's worth getting pissed off about. Don't sweat the small stuff, which is a good lesson that only took about thirty years to sink in. Not only am I not a diplomat—I'm not a fast learner, either.

Whatever anyone's understanding of things, conflicts and power struggles still went on. But I have always reserved the right to step in at crunch time and decide what to do over any and all objections. There comes a time when somebody has got to take charge, and that somebody always seems to be me. It's who I am and how I've always gotten shit done. Maybe it's just because I'm the most stubborn. Or the tallest.

Those decisions involved which gigs to take and which ones to turn down, set-list repertoire and arrangements, who should play what, and when. Being in charge also meant deciding personnel matters, who was in and who was out. Pretty much anyone who hung around for any amount of time wound up playing music with us, so there was a lot of coming and going. But the core of Asleep at the Wheel in those early years was still Lucky, Leroy, and me. We also had a new bassist, Gene Dobkin, who stepped in after our old bass player went kind of nuts on us. Madness takes its toll.

Maybe the easiest personnel decision we ever made came about after an old Mercury pulled up to our house one evening and two pretty girls got out. Chris O'Connell and Emily Paxton. Hello, young ladies. Chris and Emily were about our age and had grown up in northern Virginia, where they'd been writing songs and singing together since the age of ten. They'd seen Asleep at the Wheel open for Poco in Washington, D.C., the week before and liked our show enough to come out to the country looking for us.

At the mention of singing, our ears perked right up. Girl singers, hmm—that sounded like a highly promising addition to our sound. So we asked them to come show us what they had. We retired to the rehearsal room and fired up Willie Nelson's "Hello Walls" and Johnny Cash's "Don't Take Your Guns to Town" to test them out. My first reaction was to feel pleased that they already knew both songs, because not too many people our age did. My second reaction was to marvel that, damn, we never sounded better. They were interested in being a part of the band, so we immediately started plotting how to work them into the act. That was late fall when they showed up, and we told them to come back after Christmas.

After they came back, we had a few weeks of rehearsals before debuting Asleep at the Wheel's new backup singers at a show in lovely Rockville, Maryland, on January 8, 1971 (Elvis Presley's thirty-sixth birthday, for those keeping track). Chris and Emily were real treasures, sweetening our sound and adding another vocal dimension to the combination of my wise-guy character-actor baritone and Leroy's more traditional country voice.

Emily couldn't stay with us too long, as she had to return home after a few months and tend to family matters with her sick father. But Chris stayed on, and her voice quickly became an Asleep at the Wheel signature as we evolved into an ensemble revue with multiple lead singers. Over time, Chris blossomed into an amazing vocalist. She could belt like any big-voiced country singer you've ever heard, then change gears and glide with the greatest of ease into Sarah Vaughan's style of sultry jazz. When we started doing more songs featuring Chris on lead vocals, that's when the band truly went to the next level.

It, um, also wasn't long before Chris and I had hooked up as a couple.

As we continued on our path, it wasn't just the band that was improving. I was growing more confident as a performer, too, especially when I learned how to make use of my attention deficit disorder. The upside of ADD is I can multitask, because I'm always thinking about something else. Onstage, it's the next song we're gonna play. People always talk about being "in the moment" onstage, but I'm almost always thinking about what to do next. Although sometimes what I'm thinking about is dinner, or my foot hurting, or hoping nobody notices that I just farted. I once asked Willie Nelson if he farted on every stage.

"Yep," he said. "Every stage."

Anyway, where was I? Right—the good part of ADD.

The even better part of it is that the ADD mind often wanders off into the cosmos, where your subconscious arrives at conclusions it might take your day-to-day mind a while to catch up to. I'd started out as a mostly self-taught, purely emotional guitar player, learning things by ear and gradually picking up technical things as my chops improved. And as I became savvier about it, I came to realize that music can be broken down into math, as intervals. Every style has the same twelve notes, and the music's essence is what you do with intervals to create different dialects, accents, colors.

Take music theory, which is really nothing more than math. One, three, five, the dominant seventh, the major seventh—those are numbers related to the twelve-note scale we use in Western music, and it all comes down to what you swap out and how you put things together. First time I figured that out was on the Sportsman's Club stage in Paw Paw one night, when I was screwing around on guitar and changed the diminished to a dominant, and a lightbulb went off.

"Aha," I thought, "so *that*'s the substitution I've heard people talking about!"

By substituting in something more complex, I'd gone to where jazz and blues were. Once you realize that, the next step is to think about what else you can substitute, which is where vocabulary comes in. Minor chords come out sad and tragic, diminished chords are anticipatory; so what do you want to happen next? Whether you're playing country or classical, everything has emotional tags. What you leave out and put in determines how you'll tap into that emotion.

Now the way Al Di Meola plays is numbers and a whole lot of 'em, very fast, which is why almost nobody else can do what he does. Us lesser mortals can learn music by the numbers, memorize the mathematical relationships of notes to each other, but that's a cold, cold way to go about it. The real thing happens when you use musical math on more of an instinctual level to express pure emotion, like Kurt Cobain. He used just about the most basic math there is to get into really complicated, difficult emotions.

Seems simple, but it's genius. And while Asleep at the Wheel never played anything like Nirvana's punk rock, that kind of musical emotion is what we were after.

During our time in West Virginia, I was also in touch with our friends Commander Cody and His Lost Planet Airmen, and their manager, Joe Kerr. I'd go into town to the pay phone (remember those?) and dial him up using a phony credit card number, back in the pre-computer days when you could get away with such chicanery. Joe and I would shoot the shit about his band, my band, our plans for the future, and ways we could help each other out.

Next time Cody was due to come east, I went to one of our regular D.C. clubs, the Emergency, and made the owner an offer. I promised him that Cody would draw enough to cover the club's $300 guarantee; and if not, then we'd make up the difference with a gig. Naturally they didn't cover the cash, so Asleep at the Wheel had to make good on that. But no matter. We were making history on a shoestring, and there was no way we'd let a lousy three hundred bucks stop us.

Besides which, at that point in time, Cody was about to go big. Their first album, *Lost in the Ozone*, was coming out at the end of 1971, and they'd be in the Top 10 by summer with "Hot Rod Lincoln." And since the last time I'd seen Cody at Antioch, they had become about the rockin'-est band of freaks on the planet, up to an eight-piece lineup playing this sort of retro-rockabilly Western swing with a lot of country. To this day, I've never seen a more amazing combination of druggie outlandishness and musical precision.

Cody was living the life and I still don't know how he and his guys did it, but I was glad they were on our side. They were our comrades in a war against Nashville's slick country-pop and L.A.'s slicker country-rock. We were both outlaws by virtue of lifestyle and attitude, and we were ready to go anywhere and do anything to play our music the way we wanted to.

Of course, to do that, we had to keep everybody's vehicles running. After Cody's D.C. show, his car had a flat tire and he had no spare. It was two in the morning and no stores were open, tire or otherwise. So Cody, being a Commander and all, deputized me to go find him a tire, and I did. Right around the corner was a vehicle of similar style to his and we jacked it up, made off with a tire, and split.

So . . . to the owner of that 1968 Volkswagen sedan, wherever you are: we'd like to thank you for the loan of your left front tire, and also to apologize for any inconvenience it may have caused you back in 1971. Sorry about that. You can send the bill to George Frayne.

Seeing Cody again lit a fire in us. With their encouragement (and after consulting the I Ching, as I often do on matters requiring a decision), we decided we should move on out to California ourselves. We felt strange about leaving our nest in West Virginia, though. So much had already happened that it seemed like we'd been there a lot longer than a year and a half. Somehow, a handful of East Coast suburban kids had become real country-western folk. Well, whether or not we were "real," we certainly did look, dress, and sound the part.

It was time to move along to greener pastures and (we hoped) bigger things. So we did what pioneers have been doing since the dawn of America: we went west, young man. Woman, too, in our case. Our roadie, Ralph, traded in his car for an almost-new 1969 Ford pickup with sixteen-inch wheels and four on the floor, perfect for hauling gear. We traveled in a caravan of the pickup, Gene Dobkin's Dodge Dart, and a 1961 Cadillac I'd bought for $250. Before we left, Gene painted an Asleep at the Wheel wagon-wheel logo on all three vehicles (we still use that same logo to this day).

Yeah, we were regular Beverly Hillbilly Hippies, except we were going to Cody's hometown of Berkeley instead of Hollywood. We packed up all our instruments and provisions, including freshly cured venison jerky and a few gallons of homemade elderberry wine—but no pot or drugs, so as not to get busted on our way through Middle America.

We left West Virginia in August 1971 and stopped off in Yellow Springs to visit and say so long to some of our Antioch friends in Ohio. Even though we were going a lot farther away, they were less worried for us over this move. For a pack of long-hairs, California seemed like a friendlier destination than rural West Virginia. Still, it was a pretty crazy leap of faith we were taking. Once again, we'd packed up to move to a strange new place with no money, jobs, or prospects, and we were counting on the kindness of friends and strangers. I was twenty years old and owned not much more than that Cadillac, a couple of guitars, and miles of ambitions. Onward through the fog . . .

From Yellow Springs, we picked up Interstate 70 westbound and came to St. Louis about four hundred miles later, crossing the mighty Mississippi River. We were into the frontier, with the fruited plain spread before us leading to the Rocky Mountains, the western desert, and eventually the Pacific Ocean. Like Jack Kerouac, Scott McKenzie, and all the con men and misfits who followed the gold rush of 1849, we were bound for San Francisco.

The rest of the trip was fairly uneventful, which was a good thing because we had scraped together just enough money to make it to California barring any major mishaps. The closest thing to a crisis was when my old Cadillac started making a god-awful noise late one night around Salt Lake City. The generator was failing, so our solution was to turn the Caddy's lights off and put it between the Ford pickup and the Dodge Dart in our caravan. Worked great, except it wasn't exactly legal. A cop pulled us over to ask what in the world we were doing, and wound up letting us off with a stern warning (yes, leaving the drugs behind had been a good call). But we had to wait until daylight to continue.

We finally crossed into California, reached San Francisco, pulled over at a pay phone, and called Cody for directions. As soon as we got to Andy Stein's house in Berkeley, the Caddy died right there and never moved again.

# *On the Road Again*

EXCEPT FOR THE occasional old-time string band of real hillbillies, we were pretty much the only band around our neck of the woods in West Virginia—and certainly the only bunch of longhairs. Then when we branched out to Washington, D.C., we were no longer alone, although it still wasn't too crowded. But the San Francisco Bay Area was full to bursting with bands on the verge when we got there in the summer of 1971. There was Cody, of course, along with Tower of Power, Doobie Brothers, Joy of Cooking, and lots more. Also in the vicinity was Van Morrison, the Irish soul singer. Thanks to *Moondance*, he was just about the biggest thing on earth, living with his wife and muse, Janet Planet, across the bridge in Marin County.

Cody had originally formed in Michigan in 1967 before moving to Berkeley, and they'd been working the Bay Area circuit long enough to build a sizable following—big enough to outgrow a lot of the smaller local clubs. With Cody's blessing, we set about inheriting their slot at a lot of these places. Several of them were on University Avenue near campus, New Monk and Mandrake's. Two more were on San Pablo Avenue, the Longbranch and a folk club called Freight & Salvage. Farther afield, we had the Lion's Share over in San Anselmo; Town & Country Inn down near Santa Cruz; and up in the Sonoma County town of Sebastapol, the Inn of the Beginning.

We'd play 'em all soon enough, but started by going to the Longbranch with a proposal: entice people to come in the door with a $1 cover, which also included one free beer. Okay, they said. But it bombed the first time we tried it—a potentially dire turn of events, as we were running out of money fast. So for the second try, the band sucked it up and spent our last few dollars printing up handbills to give out on Telegraph Avenue, the main drag over by the University of California. I also pawned my Guild Firebird guitar for thirty bucks, most of which went into our pickup truck's gas tank. I never saw that old guitar again, but about forty people showed up at the Longbranch on the second try and our bacon was saved, at least for one more day. We played three sets, and by the end of the night we had the beginnings of a local fan base.

We kept at it, sharing bills with a lot of local bands and getting to know them. There were the Rockets, a band you may not have heard of. But there's a pretty good chance you've heard their lead singer, Eddie Mahoney—he goes by the name of Eddie Money as a solo act. Then there was Clover, a country-rock band from Marin County that wound up having an interesting career. Later in the '70s they went to England to get in on the "pub rock" wave of punk, but it didn't go well. Not even Robert John "Mutt" Lange, a producer of megasellers by everybody from AC/DC to Shania Twain, could get a hit out of Clover. But while they were in England, they were the backup band on *My Aim Is True*, the first album by a young punk singer named Declan MacManus—you know, Elvis Costello. After Clover came back to America, several of them started a new band called Huey Lewis and the News and hit the jackpot.

All these years later, Huey's still a golfing buddy of mine. So is his Clover bandmate John McFee, who went on to the Doobie Brothers.

Musically, we did great right out of the gate in the Bay Area. Our level of musicianship was improving by leaps and bounds, and our crowds grew bigger and bigger. But . . . we were still broker than broke and just about starving to death despite pinching every penny we could. After we'd imposed on Cody for as long as everybody could stand it, the first place of our own we got was this old shotgun-style house on East 26th Street in an Oakland neighborhood that was (pardon the political incorrectness) a ghetto. Lots of blacks and older Asians, young white hippies and bikers, and pockets of retirees here and there. And us.

Our vow-of-poverty station aside, Oakland suited us—a retro town for a retro band. There was good soul food and barbecue in the neighborhood, and it was also cheap, which was good because cheap was all we could (barely) afford. Whatever money came in went straight to rent, food, and gas, and none of us saved a dime. Our house had a living room, a kitchen, and three small bedrooms. Chris and I were in one while the other two rooms had two guys each. The basement, we used for band rehearsals.

Since we were living in a rough neighborhood and could not afford to have our instruments stolen, we got a dog to discourage burglars. A friend gave us a Weimaraner that was big, ill-tempered, and borderline unmanageable. It was perfect guard-dog material and even served as an occasional food provider (bonus!). One day that dog came trotting into the house with a paper bag from a nearby chicken place in his mouth. It was a trash bag with nothing but chicken bones, and we were all so broke and hungry that we ate them right up without a second thought. In all ways, we were literally sucking the marrow out of life, I guess.

All was well until the dog got sick and had to stay overnight at the veterinarian's. Thieves must have been keeping our freaky band house under surveillance, because by morning, they had broken into our unguarded basement and made off with Leroy's Martin D-35 acoustic and my Telecaster electric. Leroy's guitar was gone for good, but I was lucky enough to find my Telecaster at a pawnshop. Paid twenty-five bucks to get it back and kept it another twenty years—until it was stolen again in New York City.

Eventually, we scraped together the wherewithal to move to a nicer part of Oakland, a decrepit old mansion over by Lake Merritt. The mansion counted Oakland's first mayor among its former inhabitants, and it was huge—five bedrooms, big living room, quaint yard—but also in a state of serious disrepair. Whatever, it was ours for $250 a month, which gave us all the room we needed to spread out, live, and rehearse in comfort. Now we just had to make enough money to afford it.

There's a song by the group Alabama that says if you're gonna play in Texas, you've gotta have a fiddle in the band. We weren't in Texas (yet), but we decided we needed a fiddle player anyway. It would make us even more country and help Asleep at the Wheel stand out from the other bands. A fellow named Danny Levin had played fiddle with us some in West Virginia, but he hadn't made the trip out west and we still didn't have a full-time fiddler.

Andy Stein from Cody's band would sometimes sit in with us, and we liked how it sounded. So we started looking for a fiddle player of our own, and that search led us to some interesting people. One of them was Joe Burns, an old-time country fiddler who came and jammed at Cody's place in Berkeley. He sounded great with us, even though he was really just a little too old for the starving-musician trip we were on.

Joe Burns did, however, provide our introduction to one Stoney Edwards, a country singer who was black—highly unusual, both then and now. Capitol Records had signed Stoney to turn him into "the Other Charley Pride," and he was looking for a group to serve as his backup band, the Poor Folks (named after his biggest hit at that time, "Poor Folks Stick Together"). Us being quite literally poor folks—and priced to move, as they say—we fit the bill nicely. So Asleep at the Wheel got the gig with Stoney after Joe hooked us up.

Stoney's manager was Ray Sweeney, who had been in the business long enough to book Bob Wills back during his prime, and I used to pump him for stories of the old days. He'd tell some tales; also got us to dressing like one of the old bands, with country-western suits bought from Judy Lynn's band (and a dress and padded bra for Chris). Even after cutting our hair, we still looked pretty scruffy.

But the biggest thing Sweeney and Stoney did was to get Asleep at the Wheel onto our new home away from home: the road. The lot of us traveled in a jam-packed Winnebago, making the princely sum of fifty bucks a week. Still, I was in heaven—living the Yankee Jewboy hippie's dream of becoming a hillbilly musician. Since Jews and cowboys both make a big fuss about wearing hats indoors, it always made perfect sense to me.

Pot was still unusual in country circles in 1971, but we went right on smoking it—on the sly, of course. We'd be in the back of the Winnebago when we weren't driving, blowing smoke out the window. Up front, Stoney didn't even know.

Pills, however, were another matter entirely—very much the drug of choice for everybody in country music, from Johnny Cash on down to the lowliest roadie. Seemed like every picker, grinner, lover, sinner, songwriter, bus driver, and hanger-on was fueling his engine with uppers, speed, and poppers. They had names like black mollies, great speckled birds, Christmas trees, white crosses, L.A. turnarounds. There was Desoxyn, the Cadillac of speed, as well as Benzedrine, Dexedrine, Dexamyl. And when it was time to come down from all that and sleep, downers awaited: Seconal, Tuinal, Quaaludes, Valium. We quickly became accustomed to pill-popping blurs of driving six, eight, ten hours at a time in a state of semiconsciousness.

Man, it was nuts. Taking pills for days at a time, you could drink enormous quantities of booze without falling over or even slowing down. Everybody did it. Just listen to one of the songs Roger Miller wrote back then:

*Well the moon is high and so am I*
*The stars are out and so will I be pretty soon . . .*

Yeah, real pill poetry. Stoney didn't know a thing about the pot, or about all the pills we were taking to make those long drives at all hours of the might.

"You boys sure do stay up late," he'd say. Yeah, Stoney, you bet.

Seriously, though, speed really is about the safest way to drive. Asleep at the Wheel may be a funny name, but it's no joke—you've got to be alert if you're driving anything, but especially a damn bus. During World War II, they'd give what they called "combat fatigue pills" to pilots who had to fly round-the-clock sorties, and it was the best speed government money could buy.

I don't take pills like that anymore because my body just can't handle it. But if I were a late-night truck driver, I might.

Being on the road with Stoney was the beginning of my post-graduate crash-course education in country music. We'd go out for six weeks at a time and play honky-tonks, military bases, fairs, package shows where we'd back up Stoney and every other act on the bill. We learned how to play almost everything, and how to fake our way through everything else. It's a useful skill.

One of our first tours with Stoney started out in Reno, Nevada, which of course meant gambling. Everyone went in with ten bucks and we all more or less broke even—except for Stoney, who won $600 and wired it home to cover that month's Winnebago payment. You'd think a nice and unexpected little windfall like that might have loosened up the purse strings, but it did not. We were too green to know the difference anyway.

From Reno, we went five hundred miles northeast to Nampa, Idaho; then over a thousand miles southeast to New Mexico to play some military bases and honky-tonks like Glenn's Bar, a joint that gave new meaning to the phrase "out of the way." Glenn's Bar was about fifteen miles outside of Hobbs, and depending on which direction you were headed, it was in either Far East New Mexico or Far West Texas. The place had a drive-through window for booze, a bar with pool tables, and a surprisingly large room with a dance floor where bands could play for crowds in the hundreds. God only knows where they came from, when they did. The night we were there, they didn't.

"I don't know if y'all are gonna have a crowd," the waitress warned. "There was a shooting here last night."

Sure enough, maybe a dozen people showed up at Glenn's Bar

that night. But we made a $10 tip for playing "Faded Love" by request. I've always loved that song, enough to put it on two of Asleep at the Wheel's three Bob Wills tribute albums (one version features Lyle Lovett and Shawn Colvin, the other Vince Gill and the Time Jumpers).

After bombing at Glenn's Bar, we drove all night with snow blowing across Route 66, through Amarillo to Seminole, Oklahoma, to play the Circle W Corral, a BYOB ballroom that held about a thousand souls. No, you still could not buy liquor by the drink in Oklahoma in 1971, but people still managed to get plenty oiled up. One of the popular dances was the "Paul Jones," which worked like this: girls on the inside and guys on the outside, both rotating in opposite directions until the bandleader blew a whistle, whereupon whoever was in front of you was your new dance partner. If you think elbows get thrown in basketball, that's nothing compared to a crowd jockeying for position while doing the Paul Jones. And if they didn't get the partner they wanted, well, that was the band's fault and we'd hear about it.

Bless his heart, Stoney took just about everything in stride, even stuff like Chris O'Connell's almost setting his Winnebago on fire. But an even keel and the ability to just roll with it were musts if you really wanted to make it as a black country singer. For a black guy from Oklahoma like Stoney, that world was the belly of the beast. It probably helped that he was illiterate. People in the crowd would hand notes up to the stage, and Stoney passed them over to me to read. They'd say things like, "Stoney, get the hell off the stage," which was not exactly subtle. Neither was the couple I wound up talking to one night at Cain's Ballroom in Bob Wills's old stomping ground of Tulsa, Oklahoma.

"We love Charley Pride and Stoney and we're not prejudiced," the woman said. "My husband used to be. He threw out my Fats Domino records and said I was not to listen to those niggers."

"But I'm not prejudiced anymore," her husband declared proudly. Uh-huh, sure. I remember being glad the guy didn't know I was Jewish, because I'm pretty sure he wouldn't have been over that.

# Into the Mystic with "The Beatles of Western Swing"

IN THE FALL OF 1971, one of Asleep at the Wheel's tours with Stoney took us all the way to Nashville to play the big country radio Disc Jockey Convention. Every label would bring in its acts and put on showcases while wining and dining country deejays and program directors, hoping it would all result in airplay. So we backed up Stoney at the convention's Capitol Records party, and I was awestruck at the company we were keeping. The other acts on the bill included Buck Owens, Tex Ritter, and Don Rich—legends all—and the master of ceremonies was Ralph Emery, a deejay who was in the Country Music Hall of Fame. It was hard not to gawk.

As always, Stoney had us on a super-tight budget, which usually meant going hungry. But Cody, whose album was about to come out, was also in town, and their label put them up at the Sheraton Hotel. Between sponging off their free room service and a journalist with an expense account, we ate well. Kindness of friends and strangers, baby. We had a blast and even managed to make a decent impression on our own as Asleep at the Wheel.

In retrospect, that period really was the beginning of modern country music as we know it today because, for better or worse, that's when Nashville started trying to de-regionalize and de-Southernize it. We were part of the younger generation's wild-eyed freaky contingent, along with Cody, New Riders of the Purple Sage, and Dan Hicks. There was also the slicker L.A. contingent of the Byrds—the Flying Burrito Brothers, and all their spin-offs. And slicker still, acts that were less country and more pop—the Eagles, Linda Ronstadt, and Crosby, Stills & Nash.

Seemed like there should be room for Asleep at the Wheel somewhere in there, and man, did we need a break. Between tours with Stoney, we continued playing gigs back home in the Bay Area and took every one we could, including some we should've turned down. At one point, we took a regular gig playing Sunday nights at Bobby McGee's, a club attached to a truck-stop coffee shop on Highway 101. That place's main house band was called Three Jacks and an Earl, and they were. Jack Daniels, later of the hit country band Highway 101, played guitar; Jack Greenback, the drummer, used to play with Bob Wills's Texas Playboys; the pianist was named Jack Springer; and Earl, I've forgotten.

At Bobby McGee's, we were all working for a couple of characters straight out of an old black-and-white crime film. The owner was cross-eyed from a fight while the money man was an old crippled guy on crutches, and they seemed drunk most of the time. Gambling, bootlegging, and prostitution went on there, too. Tough joint.

Tough work, too. During the week, Three Jacks and an Earl played four 45-minute sets a night, which was hard enough. Weekends were even harder—they'd do eight sets a night, from nine p.m. to six in the morning. Sunday nights, they'd get a break when we played from five to nine, and then they'd take over and play again until closing time. This was before karaoke, but that's basically what it was, because anybody who wanted to could come up and sing with us. And while I can't remember how much we were making, I'm sure it wasn't enough.

Bobby McGee's wasn't the only karaoke-type gig Asleep at the Wheel has ever had. A few years later, we were the house band for a spell at the Palomino Club in L.A., which was one of those places with a bouncer named Tiny who really, really wasn't. Glen

Campbell, Bonnie Raitt, Peter Fonda, and the film critic Leonard Maltin were regulars, and a lot of Playboy Pinups, Penthouse Pets, and aspiring starlets were always hanging around. We'd play a couple nights a week and also do the Sunday-evening jam where any truck driver, wannabe urban cowboy, former choir girl, or current drunk could get up and sing.

It was often hilarious in a painful sort of way, but I remember one little girl who really could sing. She was named Christina and her mom was a nurse. They were hanging out with us one night when we were talking about Wynonie Harris, the great "dirty blues" soul shouter from the '50s who was always doing songs like "Keep on Churnin'" and "I Like My Baby's Pudding." Christina's mom asked about the spelling and said that if you changed the ending from "ie" to "a," then "Wynona" could be a girl's name.

"Well," I said, "don't forget Winona"—just me trying to be funny, quoting the song "Route 66."

Christina's mom tweaked the spelling a bit by the time they started performing together as the Judds a few years later. And that's how Wynonna Judd, one of the great voices of our time, got her stage name.

As 1972 wore on, things finally started happening. Asleep at the Wheel had gotten to the point where we could pack out pretty much anyplace we played in the Bay Area, and we were getting better as a band, too. Chris was hitting her stride as a singer, well on her way to becoming one of the greats, and Leroy, Lucky, and I were keeping up pretty well, if I say so myself. Andy Stein was a great addition on fiddle, when he wasn't busy with Cody. And we added keyboards from a California native named Jim Haber, although you know him as Floyd Domino. Having a piano in the band added yet another dimension to the sound.

Some of the right people were starting to notice us, too. One day, Van Morrison's office called out of the blue and left a message for us at Joe Kerr's house. It was an invitation for us to come visit his house in Fairfax, over in Marin County, and hell yes, we were going. Van was rock royalty. Chris and I took the pickup and went off to pay Van the Man a visit, and it was very nice. We talked about Van maybe producing Asleep at the Wheel, which didn't happen. But he did put us on a few shows with him.

While that was plenty cool and would have been more than enough, the best thing Van ever did for Asleep at the Wheel was to drop our name in a very influential place. He did an interview that ran in *Rolling Stone* magazine's June 22, 1972, issue, where he was asked if he'd seen many bands around the Bay Area since moving there. And Van, bless his heart, said this:

> Not a hell of a lot, but there's some relatively unknown groups that I really dig. Like Asleep at the Wheel plays great country music. They're really good musicians.

Van talking us up in *Rolling Stone* was what finally got record companies to pay attention to Asleep at the Wheel, and I'll always owe him a huge debt for that. We've stayed friendly over the years, and on occasion Van has borrowed players from Asleep at the Wheel for tours. And it's always been my dream to work with him in the studio someday. We went to lunch one day a few years back in Austin, Texas, to talk about me producing a country album with Van, Willie Nelson, and Merle Haggard. Willie and Merle were friends, so all I needed was for Van to commit and I'd run with it. The whole thing sounded great, and the talk was all good up until I asked Van if he still drank.

"Nah," he said. "Not for eight years. Not saying I'll never drink again. But the bad thing is, when I go out drinking, next day people expect me to do what I said I'd do."

It was at that moment I realized that no matter what he said, I would never get to produce Van Morrison. So it goes.

Getting the Van Morrison seal of approval in *Rolling Stone* seemed to open the floodgates. A few other articles ran, and suddenly Asleep at the Wheel was as close to a "hot property" as we'd ever be. The planets, it seemed, were all lining up. Cody had broken into the Top 10 with the "Hot Rod Lincoln" single, the Nitty Gritty Dirt Band had a gold album for *Will the Circle Be Unbroken*, and we had just enough of a profile for business types to imagine us being next in line. I pictured an oily showbiz guy in a bad suit and a fancy office screaming over the phone, "Get me another long-haired country-rock band with a funny name!"

All of which is to say that our phone started ringing around that time. While it never quite developed into a bidding-war situation, we did hear from a whole bunch of people from the A&R department of various labels—"A&R" standing for "Artists & Repertoire," the talent scouts who go out and find bands to sign to recording contracts.

Corporate America had not yet bought up everything, so there were still dozens of record companies out there, and it seemed like we talked to all of them: Metromedia, Atlantic, Vanguard, Capitol, even Playboy (yes, Playboy Enterprises, Inc., really did have its very own label). Every week, we'd go out to another expensive dinner with these people to talk "deals," which meant we were eating better than we ever had. The labels also financed "demos," recordings you'd make to show off your songs and abilities. They'd write us a check, we'd record it on the cheap and pocket the difference. We still weren't getting rich, but at least we weren't starving.

The one we eventually signed with was United Artists Records, mostly because their A&R guy, Dan Bourgoise, just went so crazy for us and we figured that couldn't hurt. Dan called Asleep at the Wheel "the Western swing Beatles" and said that seeing us made him feel like he was watching Bob Wills and the Texas Playboys in a roadhouse somewhere. The Beatles thing still makes me laugh all these years later, but I did like hearing the Bob Wills comparison.

Dan managed Del Shannon—*the* Del Shannon, of "Runaway" fame, who I'd been hearing on the radio since I was a kid—and brought him in to help us make a demo. Del was an enthusiastic fellow, telling anyone who would listen that he loved Asleep at the Wheel because we were "REAL country music, not that watered-down Nashville shit!" Amen, brother. Del remained a supportive and loyal friend up until his sad death by suicide in 1990. Somewhere in my office, I still have a telegram that Del once sent us right before a show we did in Hollywood: "Sorry I can't make your Palomino date. I know you'll kill 'em."

By the fall of 1972, the deal was done, and Asleep at the Wheel was a United Artists recording act. We would have been happy to get the $5,000 we were expecting, but we somehow wound up getting a $25,000 advance plus a $20,000 recording budget. High cotton, baby. We also hired Joe Kerr, who was still handling Cody and also New Riders of the Purple Sage (of "Panama Red" fame) to manage us. We returned to the country radio Disc Jockey Convention to do our own showcase and preview songs from our debut album. Titled *Comin' Right at Ya*, it was scheduled to come out in early 1973.

When Asleep at the Wheel went to record the "official" version of our first album, we were looking for a producer and found a good one in Tommy Allsup, who came at the recommendation of fiddler Buddy Spicher. Tommy's a man who has lived a charmed life, going back to a coin flip he lost in 1959. On February 3 of that year, an airplane was about to leave Clear Lake, Iowa. There was one seat left, and both Tommy and Ritchie "La Bamba" Valens wanted it. So those two flipped a coin, Valens won, and you know the rest. It was "The Day the Music Died." The plane crashed shortly after takeoff and everyone onboard died, including Valens, Buddy Holly, and J. P. "The Big Bopper" Richardson.

Allsup was in Holly's Crickets, and another lucky Cricket that night was Waylon Jennings. He'd taken pity on Richardson because the Bopper had a cold, so Waylon gave him his seat. That saved Waylon's life at the age of twenty-one and he went on to have a fantastic career, peaking in the late 1970s when he and Willie Nelson sang about getting back to the basics of love and feelin' no pain down in Luckenbach, Texas. Waylon passed away in 2002 from complications of diabetes. Asleep at the Wheel played a show with him in Chicago about six months before the end, and he needed a big-type teleprompter for the words because his eyes and memory weren't working too great. But

Waylon still sang so beautifully, it was hard to imagine him ever being gone. After he was, *USA Today*'s obituary writer called me for a quote and I said, "I didn't think he'd die."

As for Tommy Allsup, on the twenty-year anniversary of his Clear Lake near miss, he would open a club in Fort Worth called Tommy's Heads Up Saloon in honor of the night he tossed that fifty-cent piece (which he still had all those years later). Back in the day, Tommy had gone on to work with Roy Orbison and our idol, Bob Wills. So he seemed like the perfect producer for Asleep at the Wheel, and he did get a mighty fine record out of us.

Fittingly, side one of *Comin' Right at Ya* started with a little Bob Wills, our loose version of his standard "Take Me Back to Tulsa." We also covered Hank Williams's "I'll Never Get Out of This World Alive," Moon Mullican's "Cherokee Boogie," and Hank Snow's "I've Been Everywhere" as done by Johnny Cash (a singer I'd been imitating for years). But the majority of the album's twelve songs were originals, and Leroy had a hand in writing most of them.

For the cover, we posed in the Western suits we'd worn with Stoney, gathered together in a sort of cheerleader-looking formation in which everybody except me had hands outstretched. I was in the back, so I didn't tower over everybody else as much as usual. And while our hair didn't look too long in the cover shot, well, it wasn't really short enough, either.

Between the countercultural glee-club feel on the cover and the old-fashioned honky-tonk vibes in the grooves, *Comin' Right at Ya* seemed to confuse lots of folks in and out of the country-music audience. Neither side exactly took to us. Admittedly, we were pretty much all over the place, with three very different singers in Leroy, Chris, and me (four, if you counted Gene doing his vocal star turn on "I've Been Everywhere"). So who were we? A straight-up country-western band with a girl singer who had an amazing voice? A song-based ensemble led by a conventional singer-songwriter? Or a Western swing revival outfit fronted by a freaky-tall deep-voiced guy?

We were all that and more, which made for fun and lively shows but also meant it was hard for the industry to pigeonhole us the way it always tries to do. Not surprisingly, Nashville in general and country radio in particular didn't know quite what to make of us. This wasn't too many years after Roger McGuinn had seen a copy of the Byrds' *Sweetheart of the Rodeo* album tacked up on a bulletin board at a country radio station with an ugly message written on the cover: "Do not play. This is not country music." While I never saw anything like that with Asleep at the Wheel, I'll bet that *Comin' Right at Ya* got a similar reaction from most of the powers that be.

Oddly enough, one of the best reviews we got was in that noted country-music hotbed, New York City, which was weird. And it was in the city's alternative paper, the *Village Voice*, which was even weirder. The rock columnist Robert Christgau awarded *Comin' Right at Ya* an A-minus—my best grade of any sort in years, in or out of school—with a review that probably gave us more credit than we deserved:

> Their coterie complains about flat recording and performance, but flatness is of the essence in Western swing, and the sly singing and positively underhanded songwriting here exploit it brilliantly. Beneath their unflappable veneer these country revisionists are seething subversives; it may even be that the protagonist of "Daddy's Advice" only plans his little murder to right a case of incest. Side one ends with a song of praise to a spaceship. Side two ends with a song of praise to the Son of God.

Finally, somebody who got where we were coming from, seething subversiveness and all. But while that was great to see, it didn't do us a lick of good with country radio—or United Artists Records, for that matter. Our stay there was a short one. Neither of the singles released from *Comin' Right at Ya* made the charts and the album didn't sell, so they dropped us.

Yeah, Beatles of Western swing, my ass.

# *Austin Calling*

AFTER *COMIN' RIGHT AT YA* ran its course, Asleep at the Wheel went through some lineup changes. Probably the biggest was Leroy moving out from behind the drums. Since he was one of our main songwriters and singers, it made sense for him to be out front on guitar alongside Chris and me. Scott Hennige stepped in to replace him on drums. As for the other half of the rhythm section, Gene Dobkin left after playing on the album, and his replacement was a teenager named Tony Garnier, whose grandfather led brass bands in New Orleans. Tony would stay with us until the late '70s and eventually wind up in Bob Dylan's band. Finally, after borrowing Lost Planet Airmen fiddle player Andy Stein to play on the first album, we brought our old West Virginia friend Danny Levin out to be Asleep at the Wheel's full-time fiddler.

With a lineup set, the next task was to find another record deal. And here is where I feel like I really earned my keep as Asleep at the Wheel's bandleader: I'm good at the hustle and I'm also good at the schmooze, better than just about anyone I know. Always have been, because it comes naturally (thanks, Dad!).

But I've worked at it, too. Over the years, I've kind of perfected hanging out as an art form. Hanging out and being a mastermind bandleader might be my two best skills. Being open to people from all walks of life, and willing to see the good in them, have stood me well, too. As I've discovered, most folks really do have an interesting side. Might not be obvious at first, so drawing it out of them might take some effort—but it's just about always there if you're willing to spend the time to get to it.

I've spoken at a lot of colleges about entrepreneurial marketing and how to go about promoting your "brand," whether it's music or something else. The most important part of that is networking, which is nothing more than hanging out with the people you want to be like. Whether it's joining the country club to get into the same foursome as the CEO of a company you want to work for or selling pot to get a gig, it's kind of the same principle. Hanging out was part of our job with Asleep at the Wheel, even when we weren't playing a show. Either we were jamming, seeing someone else play, seeing a girl, getting drunk, getting high, or all of the above. Whatever it took to try and wind up at the right place at the right time to meet someone who could help us out. As I've discovered on more than one occasion, the back door is often a better way in than the front door. But always remember that while a lot of it *is* who you know, you've also gotta know enough to be able to make yourself useful once you get the right person's attention.

I really do think the world would be a much happier place if more people would just try to be, you know, *nicer*. There are some Asleep at the Wheel alumni who might find that statement funny coming from me, and I can't deny having my assholish moments—after all, everybody does. But for the most part, I like everybody and try to treat them with respect, from the people I'm playing onstage with to the folks taking drink orders out in the crowd. I've got no use for cliques and I can get along with almost anybody, even people I don't agree with about much of anything. George W. Bush, for example. Known and liked him for many years, since before he was in politics; still a good friend, he had us to the White House—and I've always thought he absolutely should not have been president, no way no how. He knows I didn't vote for him, but it doesn't mean that he and I don't get along, then or now.

Still, if you think politics are tribal, try the freakin' music business, which is overflowing with misfits, geniuses, hucksters, jivers, and too many outright frauds to count. Despite it all, somehow great things do happen at least some of the time. But it can be an ugly, brutal world, especially in the upper reaches.

A friend of mine named John Draper worked for everybody from Dr. Hook to Journey in the '70s, then the Jacksons' Victory Tour in the '80s, then Prince—who he never met despite working for him for a year—and finally Madonna. He was the poor bastard she was yelling at all the time in that movie *Truth or Dare*, during which time she also punched him in the stomach. A year later, he'd had enough and quit the circus.

Another friend, Joel Dorn, produced Roberta Flack, Leon Redbone, Bette Midler, and lots of others over the years. He came away from the experience with psychic scars a mile wide.

"Ray," Joel once told me, "rock 'n' roll is a horrible place with the worst people in the world. If you want to turn yourself into a one-name superstar, the only way to do that is to hate someone."

Even down toward my end of the food chain, it seems like we can't get out of our own way too much of the time. People in music seem to thrive on the Cult of Minor Differences, which holds that the more alike we are, the bigger those small differences between us become. I think it was Freud who came up with that, one o' them smart Jews. Whoever thought it up, it's right on the money, because a lot of people in music seem to regard success with something between disdain and fear. I even wrote a song about it once: "The Smaller the Potatoes, the Bigger the Beef."

In recent years, there's been this one band that shall remain nameless—another Western swing–type group that ought to be our best buds. We love Bob Wills and they do, too, so what's to disagree about? But because Asleep at the Wheel doesn't do every little thing exactly the way they think it should be done, that makes us the devil. Now, sometimes, similarly inclined bands do help each other out. But when they don't, look out, because it's eat-your-young time, especially with bands just starting out.

That's when they'll come up with these dumb-ass rules about what's cool, not cool, acceptable. You know, it's only cool if you wear flannel, play vintage instruments (or new instruments), or do this, that, or the other.

Worrying about crap like that is just a stupid waste of time. The way I look at it is that we're all of us crazy out here and ain't none of us getting rich—not really, compared to the super-wealthy—so everybody might as well just relax and enjoy the ride. The cosmos is so infinitely unfathomable and we're all just specks, so why sweat the small stuff? Being a good sport not only helps keep the bitterness in check, it also brings good things your way. I'm a firm believer in the idea that you get back what you put out there. Burn bridges in showbiz, and they tend to stay that way. It's a lot easier to get out than to get back in.

Between Joe Kerr's efforts and my boundless wit and charm, Asleep at the Wheel bounced back fairly quickly from United Artists' giving us the old heave-ho. We soon wound up on a new label, Epic Records—signed by the president of the label, no less, a fellow named Don Ellis. We were back in business.

The other major thing that happened as 1973 turned into 1974 was that we up and moved again, for what turned out to be the last time. Asleep at the Wheel had done well in the Bay Area, definitely kicking things up a notch during our time there. But it still never felt like our final destination. And after touring all over with Stoney and on our own, it was the wide-open spaces of Texas that seemed to suit us best of all, fittingly enough. After all, there's a reason Bob Wills called his band the Texas Playboys.

We'd met Doug Sahm in the Bay Area, and he was whispering in our ear about how we should move to Austin. So was Willie Nelson (who we'd played with a good bit by then). Willie told us we belonged there, and it seemed like good advice—especially when he told us that if we moved to Texas, we would be in high demand.

"Hell," Willie said, "if you can play 'Cotton Eye Joe' and 'Fraulein,' you can work all week."

The final nudge, once again, came from our old friends Commander Cody and His Lost Planet Airmen. We'd first played Austin with them in February 1973 at the Armadillo World Headquarters and returned there with them that November, when they recorded a weekend of shows for their album *Live from Deep in the Heart of Texas*. Whenever we walked into the Armadillo, it just felt like home.

So that was it: Asleep at the Wheel was Texas-bound, pulling up the stakes and moving to Austin. We had a new hometown to go with our new record company.

By then, the road had hardened us into a loud and proud onstage beast capable of standing up to almost anything. Wynonna Judd once said Asleep at the Wheel was like the circus, and we were, because we had to be. It didn't take us long to figure out that we'd have to do a lot more than just play to win rock crowds over with country music. One night, we were playing a bar in Baltimore and just dying—nothing happening, we were losing people, the air going out of the room. So I yelled over at Lucky, "Do something!" And what Lucky did was to get up from his steel guitar and start dancing like an absolute madman. The crowd went nuts, and it became a regular part of the show.

Sometimes at bigger places, Lucky would go climbing up the speakers and even up into rafters, which would piss off road crews, bouncers, and barmaids. But we had to have that rock 'n' roll mentality, because we were up against loud rock bands hollering about gettin' it on. I respect that, but it's not what we were built for. So we compensated with showmanship; Lucky would dance, I'd juggle and play guitar behind my head, we all told a lot of jokes.

Buddy Miller, who almost joined us in the '80s but went his own way instead, told me once that Asleep at the Wheel sometimes felt dangerous when we really got going because we were "playing music people had no idea how to move to." And Emmylou Harris described us as being like one of those old black-and-white cartoons where everything in the store comes to life late at night, playing music and swaying.

Mostly, we just wanted to make it fun for everybody, us and the crowd alike. We always took the music super-seriously, but we hated the bands that were so damn super-serious about themselves that they'd just stare at the ground. Where we really ran into that was at bluegrass festivals. Most of the audiences there liked us fine, but the puritanical types from the musical border patrol would be sniffing, "Not only are they not bluegrass, they're not even really Western swing."

Yeah, no shit, Sherlock.

We arrived in Austin during the winter of 1973–74, a time when it was a laid-back cosmic-cowboy paradise for refugees fleeing the big city. Seemed like all the twangy misfits from New York, Nashville, and L.A. were headed there. Austin had kind of a gulf between the hippie cowboy bands and the blues bands, but not in my head. I wanted Asleep at the Wheel to bridge that gap, with blues and rhythm and blues as part of what we did.

The Armadillo was the center of the scene in Austin, a big barn of a concert hall/beer garden just across the river from downtown. It was an old abandoned armory that had been turned into a 1,500-capacity concert hall, and just about everybody who was anybody played there when it was open during the '70s. Willie was a regular, as were a lot of locals, but the Armadillo was also big with the touring acts coming through town. That Bruce Springsteen guy played there on his way up, before anybody knew who he was. And the Armadillo was one of Van Morrison's favorite places in America, especially because of the shrimp enchiladas.

Asleep at the Wheel played our first gig as a local band at Palmer Auditorium, a firefighter benefit on a bill with Hank Thompson and our man Ernest Tubb. We started working the local circuit, which included the Armadillo as well as Soap Creek Saloon and Castle Creek. We quickly worked up to being a decent local draw, but we were still flat-on-our-ass broke, even after getting another record deal. Chris and I were living in a house with some friends in North Austin, off Rundberg Lane, and we kept getting our power turned off because we couldn't afford to pay the electric bill. Our neighbors took pity and were kind enough to let us plug an extension cord into one of their outlets to keep our refrigerator going (thanks, Bob and Carmen!).

Despite our continued poverty, we found Austin a groovy place to be. Rent was cheap and pot cheaper still, and good music, beautiful women, and great barbecue were everywhere. Austin was the cultural capital of the Southwest and one of the hubs of America's underground railroad—a post-hippie and pre-yuppie conglomerate of musicians, dope dealers, legislators, and college types with Texas's finest beatniks, artists, writers, and raconteurs all mixed together in an almost rural small-town setting. All of us had two things in common: total disrespect for the established order and a healthy appetite for life as defined by wine, women, and song. It was a scene like no other. The filmmaker Richard Linklater captured a lot of Austin's oddball vibe with his movie *Slacker*, which was filmed in the late '80s and caught the tail end of the old Austin.

Everybody's version of the old or "real" Austin ended the day after they got to town, and they wonder why it's not there anymore. Well, it done got bulldozed from too many people wanting in on the fun and moving there. It's still a great place I'll always love, and I have a hard time picturing myself anyplace else because I've just got too many friends here to leave. But it's changed a lot and kind of priced itself out of the market for most artists and musicians, even if a lot of the same old-timers like me are still hanging around.

Some years back, when high tech was in the midst of one of its booms, I was asked to come speak at a business conference. The discussion leader was Michael Dell, founder/CEO of Dell computers and one of the richest billionaires on earth; he likes me because I'm the only Jewish cowboy he knows. Anyway, I was asked about the difference between Austin then and now.

"Well," I said, "in 1973, we used to come to Austin to drop acid. Now we drop antacid."

Hey, they asked. Dell turned about three sheets of white. But it's true. Saying that was probably what got me into the Austin Music Awards Hall of Fame.

Meanwhile, it was time for us to make the second Asleep at the Wheel album. We'd gotten on well with Tommy Allsup and wanted him to produce us again. But Don Ellis decided instead to put us with Norro Wilson, a collaborator of Billy Sherrill—producer behind George Jones and Tammy Wynette, and the man who pretty much invented Nashville's countrypolitan sound. Norro was a slick Music Row type of the sort we were inclined to distrust, and yet he turned out to be a good fellow, a real music guy who knew bands from having played in them himself. If the label thought a slick producer would get a slick record out of Asleep at the Wheel, they were mistaken.

We recorded in Nashville, surrounded by history. We were in Columbia's Studio B, hallowed ground where Owen Bradley had developed so much of the Nashville sound. Bob Dylan, Johnny Cash, Ray Price, and Sonny James had all recorded there before. George and Tammy were in the house the same time as us, and so was Charlie Rich.

While doing overdubs upstairs in Columbia's Studio A, I started learning the ropes of how to produce. There were times when Norro was busy elsewhere and couldn't make it, so I was deputized to oversee things in his absence. I did not mind a bit, and the recording turned out really well, too.

This was our self-titled 1974 album, the cover of which showed all seven of us leaning against a 1936 Cadillac and wearing vintage Western shirts; mine was a copy of a shirt worn by Gene Autry in one of his movies. You couldn't buy that stuff back then, except the custom-made Nudie Cohn suits that were way too expensive for us. So Floyd Domino's girlfriend, Susan Penn, made them. I remember it was a hundred degrees in the shade and I was tired from driving the bus all day, which was probably why I'm yawning in that picture.

Still, *Asleep at the Wheel* was a jumpy and energetic little record where we really broadened the range of what we could do. Yes, we covered classic country tunes by Hank Penny and Cindy Walker, but also Count Basie, Fats Domino, and Louis Jordan. I thought the Fats song we did, "I'm Gonna Be a Wheel Someday," was pretty sly. Kind of a theme song.

This time around, Epic even had some sales with the album's second single, a twanged-up Western-swing remake of Louis Jordan's "Choo Choo Ch'Boogie" (a song that's still a regular part of Asleep at the Wheel's live set forty-plus years later). As usual, radio couldn't be bothered, but the single sold enough copies to make *Billboard*'s country chart and rise to number 69. Sales were especially strong in Austin, Houston, and Dallas.

We were the toast of Texas.

First full band publicity shot once we were in California. Suits bought from the Judy Lynn Band. Smile! (L-R) Chris O'Connell, Gene Dobkin, Floyd Domino, me, Leroy Preston, Lucky Oceans. Courtesy of Ray Benson.

Chris O'Connell and me at the famous Cain's Ballroom in Tulsa, Oklahoma, sometime in the 1970s. Courtesy of Ray Benson.

01019
GEN. ADM.
SEPT. 5, 1973

Armadillo World Headquarters
presents
ASLEEP
AT THE WHEEL
Armadillo World Headquarters

| Austin, Texas<br>Wednesday Eve.<br>8:00 P.M. | SEPTEMBER<br>5<br>1973 |
|---|---|

$2.00
ADVANCE

GEN. ADM.
01019
ASLEEP-WHEEL
DOOR

$2.50
SEPT. 5, 1973

Finally headlining the Armadillo. Cheap tickets!
Courtesy of Ray Benson.

My 1961 Cadillac, which got us from West Virginia to California and died in our backyard in Oakland. (L-R) Me, Leroy Preston, Floyd Domino, Gene Dobkin, Lucky Oceans, Chris O'Connell. Courtesy of Ray Benson.

Former Wheel members Tony Garnier and Cindy Cashdollar with Bob Dylan and me in Hawaii. Courtesy of Ray Benson.

I love Dolly! Courtesy of Ray Benson.

Top · Austin's finest. (L-R) Mike Judge, Turk Pipkin, Ann Richards, me, and Kinky Friedman. Courtesy of Ray Benson.

Left · Lyle and I still collaborate after all these years, both with less hair! Courtesy of Ray Benson.

Top · My 1969 Harley, driving by the Armadillo in 1976. Courtesy of Ray Benson.

Left · 6'7" and 190 pounds in 1976. Courtesy of Ray Benson.

Me and George Strait, a great talent and friend, early 1980s. Courtesy of Ray Benson.

Me and Lucky dancing. “Asleep at the Wheel was like watching a circus” —Wynonna. Courtesy of Ray Benson.

Brother Ray and Brother Ray in 1989 for an R&B Foundation event. Photo by Chuck Pulin.

The Four G's in 1961, and I sang soprano. (L-R) Me, my sister Sandy, Debbie Levinson, Tim Peck. Courtesy of Ray Benson.

Calendar that records gigs and monies paid. Notice the dollar figures. That was for the whole band! Steve Miller, Clover, etc. We still play Freight & Salvage. Courtesy of Ray Benson.

This was from the photo shoot for our second album, taken in Arlington, Texas. It was 102 degrees. (L-R) Tony Garnier, Richard Cassanova, Lucky Oceans, Chris O'Connell, me, Floyd Domino, Leroy Preston. Courtesy of Ray Benson.

The best friend a man could have! Photo by Lisa Pollard.

My first pair of custom boots from Nudie!
Courtesy of Ray Benson.

Me and Chris O'Connell with Peter Fonda at the Palomino Club in L.A. after finishing music for *Wanda Nevada* with Peter and Brooke Shields. Courtesy of Ray Benson.

Emmylou Harris sitting in at the Palomino. Courtesy of Ray Benson

WASHINGTON STAR - 1972

## ASLEEP AT THE WHEEL

# A Genuine Country Band

By WILLIAM HOLLAND
*Star Staff Writer*

**ASLEEP AT THE WHEEL**
*"None of that pretty boy crooning"*

Asleep At The Wheel, friend, is a country band. Not country-pop and not country-rock. Just country. The kind people used to listen to on juke boxes in honky tonks and truck stops 10, 15 years ago.

The kind of music Nashville became famous for, before it began to get slick, discovering the way to the big market and the big dollar was down the smooth road of pop-oriented pap with strings and things.

No, sir, old buddy, Asleep At The Wheel is the genuine article, and it took a bunch of longhaired college dropouts, five dedicated young city boys, to show that this honest American music is nothing to be ashamed of in the 1970s.

Their sound? None of that razor-cut hairdo, pretty boy crooning with their Phoenix this and Wichita that; none of that folksy professionally-clean stuff.

No, these people singing and playing through their consciously wrought time warp produce a sound that makes you believe you're sitting in some seedy bar booth with a row of empty draft beer schooners lined up in front of you, sitting and listening to the bonk and clink of a pinball machine and the band's swinging, and sometimes oh-so-sad, songs of hard times and love gone bad.

The musicians in the band don't come from Washington: in fact, they don't even live in the area. But when they do leave their country farmhouse in rural Paw Paw, West Va., Washington has been their city base of operations.

**Began In Teens**

"I really don't know why we're in Washington," Ray Benson said at their recent concert at Montgomery College in Rockville. Guitarist-singer Benson is a towering, good-natured extrovert with shoulder-length, carrot-red hair and a scorching vocabulary to match.

"Good as any other city, I guess," drummer-singer Leroy Preston replied.

Most of the band members began playing music in their early teens, usually in neighborhood rock and roll bands. All of them bypassed the folk-music approach that most suburban teens interested in country music follow. Benson actually started off his country-western ventures as a boy in an amateur square dance band.

"Few years ago, me and Lucky Oceans here played country blues, and I guess we played in rock and roll bands back in, oh, eighth grade," Benson said. "It didn't feeel right."

Lucky Oceans is the moniker of one Rueben Gossfield, a gentle young man with a deep voice and a sad Mediterranean face that defies time and place. It seems right that he plays the whining pedal steel guitar, perhaps the most Eastern of all Western musical instruments.)

Ray and Lucky met quite a few years back in Philadelphia, their home town. They ran across Leroy (who they call Lee) in Boston two years ago.

Lee is the only farm boy, and comes from Barre, Vt. "'Granite capitol of the world," several of the other band members added, as if on cue. Lee grew up with older brothers who played a lot of Elvis and Jerry Lee Lewis as well as pure hillbilly music. That's how he got country music fever.

Checkerboard Lewis, their fingers-on-fire piano player, also comes from Philadelphia, and, until recently, was Columbia University philosophy student Daniel Levin.

"Checkerboard's never played in a band before," Ray said.

Checkerboard was reading a well worn copy of Genet's "Funeral Rites" and scribbling notes in the back. He paused and said: "I studied cello all my life."

Didn't he even play piano at parties? "No, just at home," he said, and returned to his book.

"He's an egghead," Ray teased in a booming voice. "Thinks he's smart."

"That's because I am smart," Checkerboard quietly replied, stopping in mid-scribble. Everybody laughed.

His piano playing style is more like rag and stride than bluesy or rock-touched, and comes eerily close to the "country swing" style of the late forties and fifties.

"And Dick Fitzhugh here, he just came by two weeks ago," Ray went on, introducing everyone. "We've had trouble with rock bass players; they all want to play too loud and think country bass is too simple."

→

The first write-up about the band. *Washington Star*, 1971. Courtesy of Ray Benson.

# *On the Bus*

BY THE END OF 1974, things were humming along pretty well in our world. Asleep at the Wheel was coming up on five years together as a band, selling some records, opening for some big names. And we even had a business office that was actually doing a little business. We started working on getting incorporated for tax purposes and such. You know, just trying to give as little of our hard-earned money to the taxman as possible, same as any other citizen.

We were out on the road a lot, too—which is to say, by the side of it a good bit. Nowadays, Asleep at the Wheel tours in a nice forty-five-foot Prevost Motorcoach with radial tires, reliable heat and air, Internet, front lounge, back lounge, bunk beds (one of them specially made extra long for the tall cowboy), and all the other modern conveniences. Come by the bus when we're in your town and you'll probably find me sitting at my front-lounge table and rolling a joint, looking for the ball game on the satellite TV, and brewing up a java jolt in the espresso machine.

Robbie Robertson was in *The Last Waltz* whining about how the road'll kill ya because the Band did ten whole years of touring. Robertson wrote some great songs, but he's a wimp; I've done forty-five years and still going. I'm a road dog, most at home on the bus, which I've always preferred to limos and airplanes even though bus years can be like dog years—every year on the bus is like seven years off of it. So it's important that my bus is a comfortable place to be, and it is.

Back in the day, 'twas not always thus. We bought Asleep at the Wheel's first touring bus in 1973, an old forty-foot double-decker Scenicruiser from the Greyhound Bus Company. We couldn't really afford the $13,500 we paid, and I should have realized it was worn out or Greyhound wouldn't have been selling it. Let's just say its reliability was less than a hundred percent; and even when it was running, the heat didn't work in the winter and the A/C didn't work in the summer. So we were always freezing or frying on that bus, which made touring a grandly uncomfortable (mis)adventure. I remember one stretch where it was burning and leaking so much oil, we went through almost a hundred quarts in five hundred miles. Ninety-nine quarts of oil on the wall . . .

I taught myself how to drive that bus and learned how to be on-the-spot roadside mechanic for our frequent breakdowns, nursing that old thing through a couple hundred thousand miles a year. Sometimes we'd try to hire somebody else, but most of the drivers we could afford were even worse than I was—like the guy who drove us from Altoona, Pennsylvania, to somewhere down south all night with the damn emergency brake on. So I figured I might as well save us the trouble and expense and just do it myself, which meant I was driving Asleep at the Wheel in more ways than one.

I usually do okay with driving the bus so long as I'm going forward and don't have to back up. I'm sure there's a metaphor in there somewhere; I drive a bus like a shark swims, always moving ahead and not back. I've been doing it for such a long time that nothing really scares me anymore, even when it maybe should. I've been accused of being a little, oh, cavalier about not turning around.

A year after we got that Scenicruiser, we were driving through a thick Tennessee fog and hit a pileup on the highway; smashed into a little old lady and a semi. Everybody was fine, but it ripped off the right front of the bus and popped out a window. We rigged it enough to get moving again and rolled into Chicago with snow blowing in. That's as cold as cold gets.

In recent years, our regular driver, Mack, has handled the bus driving for Asleep at the Wheel, and he does a very fine job. Things were a little dicier in the old days. Once in Seattle, the driver we'd hired showed up drunk after the gig, so I had to fire him and take over the driving from there. We were on these mountain roads and I managed to put us in a ditch, leaning over with the onboard stereo hanging from cords right above poor Chris O'Connell (who was almost six months pregnant). They had to send a school bus to pick us up so we'd make the gig. Sorry about that, everybody.

Another guy we hired back then was this former marine who was all pumped up like Popeye or something. We were going from Austin to Houston, Popeye got us on the wrong highway and I yelled at him. He got all pissed off, we had words and agreed we were gonna settle it by fighting. So he pulled the bus over and hopped out, and I slammed the door behind him, locked it, got behind the wheel, and drove us to Houston myself—on the right damn road, Highway 71, like God intended. That was pretty classic, although our drummer David Sanger said he was hoping for the fight. Smart-ass. Can't believe I've let that guy stay in the band for so long.

But the one who took the cake was Punkin, a Tulsa native who used to be our bus driver, and I still don't know how we lived through it. He did a long stretch with us before going on to work for Johnny Rodriguez and then Dwight Yoakam. Some years after that, I wound up on *The Tonight Show* alongside Dwight and Angelina Jolie, and all Jay Leno wanted to talk about was Punkin—that's how much of a legend the guy was. I didn't say much because, man, most of the stuff I knew about Punkin was not exactly fit for network television.

Asleep at the Wheel always traveled on a bus full of substances, as it were, and Punkin was fuel to the fire (even though he himself was a drinker, not a pot smoker or pill popper). Hotel rooms were torn apart, inappropriate behavior with female fans occurred, and mistakes were made. Big ones, little ones, all kinds; just general all-around lunacy, almost always with Punkin involved. With him driving, we were like Unhinged at the Wheel.

After a while, Punkin also became road manager (that's how fucked up I was, trusting him to collect money). At the end of one year, my accountant came to me and said, "Ray, Punkin has not turned in any receipts for . . . oh, let's see . . . the last six months." Punkin came up with two shopping bags full of receipts, we tried to figure it out and at the end of it he tried to tell me I owed him $6,000. Uh, no. We were always on cash because the credit cards we had were maxed out. There was one night at Lake Tahoe when he came out of our gig at Harrah's with $5,000 cash. Next morning, I asked where Punkin was and somebody said, "Gambling." He'd gotten drunk and spent all night and into the morning losing our $5,000, and he was trying to win it back. Claimed he did, but to this day I have no idea.

Once in Chicago, Punkin opened the door at a stoplight to scream at the car next to us, "*We got drugs and whores on this bus*!" Just our luck, he'd chosen a plainclothes cop in an unmarked car to yell at. After pulling us over, the cop walked on, took one look at us—and yes, we'd been doing lots and lots of drugs, all of us—and said, "This is a bus of iniquity." I couldn't argue with him, and I figured we'd be on our way to jail soon. But no.

"The only reason I'm not taking you downtown," the cop said, "is I'd be filling out papers for a month. Now get the fuck outta here."

Whew! Saved by the paperweight.

Stuff like that would happen about once a week with Punkin, but not everything was his fault. Once we had early bus call and we were all onboard at five thirty in the morning, waiting on our piano player. By the time he finally showed up, I was mad enough to give him a serious beatdown. But somebody else had already done the job for me—he limped on with his nose all taped up. Apparently, he'd been screwing somebody else's wife and got caught, and the husband busted his nose. The rest of that tour sucked for him.

Then there was the time we were on tour with Johnny Paycheck and Tanya Tucker, and there were two gals hanging out after the show one night. They were both pretty good-looking and it seemed to be going well, so I asked them back to my hotel room. But once we got there, it soon became apparent that nothing was going to happen. Okay, fine. So I paraphrased Dylan—you know, "If you gotta go, go now, or else you got to stay all night," if you know what I mean—and asked them to leave. And they said no. Oh, man. There was a bit of a scene and I finally had to force them out and close the door behind them. But they weren't done with me. Next morning, we went out to the bus in the hotel parking lot and discovered that those girls had taken a hatchet and broken every single window. We rolled up to the next stop looking like we'd driven through a war, and Johnny and Tanya took one look and asked what the hell happened.

"Well," said the crew, "Ray did something to piss off two girls."

Still, Mother Nature was responsible for the biggest (or at least the most expensive) bus-related catastrophe in Asleep at the Wheel's history. In May 1980, we were touring the Pacific Northwest in the midst of a very rough stretch. Our fiddle player, Danny Levin, had quit earlier in the tour. Then Punkin's father died and he had to go back home to Tulsa. That left me driving the bus through Washington State. We passed by Mount St. Helens and saw a little smoke coming out through the snow on top; we'd heard talk about how an eruption was coming but didn't give it much thought once it was out of sight.

About 350 miles later, we got to Spokane at about eight thirty in the morning. I got out of the bus and heard a distant *whoomp*. "Hmm," I thought, "they must be blasting for construction around here." I'd been driving all night, so I went to sleep as soon as we got to our hotel. When I woke up, my first thought was that I'd slept through the gig because it was pitch-black outside. No, it was two in the afternoon and something like snow was coming down. Except it wasn't snow; it was volcanic ash. Mount St. Helens had blown up and caused a landslide that knocked a thousand feet off the top of the mountain, killed fifty-seven people, and leveled every house, bridge, and road in the vicinity. I don't even want to think what might have happened if it'd blown when we were driving by. Ashes were falling halfway across the country, but they were especially thick in Washington State.

We played the gig in Spokane while ashes were falling, and we were trapped in that hotel for a few days because the air was too thick to drive through. Finally, we decided we had to get the hell out even though there was still a ton of ash in the air. Getting from Spokane to Seattle took twice as long as usual, partly from going the long way and partly from having to stop every few hours to empty a shopping bag full of dust out of the bus's air filter. Finally, we got to Seattle, continued on with the tour, and everything seemed okay . . .

. . . Until a few weeks later, when every speaker and amplifier we had blew out because of all the silica that had gotten inside the cones. But that wasn't even the half of it. Shortly after that, the bus engine just flat blew up. It was a total meltdown, every bearing in the motor ground down, also courtesy of Mount St. Helens volcano dust. I figured it all out, and the total damage came to more than $25,000—at a lean time when we could ill afford it.

Oh well. Them's the breaks.

# *Spinning Texas Gold*

BETWEEN BUS MISHAPS, we were busy working up songs for the all-important third Asleep at the Wheel album, which we figured we'd be recording soon for Epic Records. Record executives come and go with dizzying speed, and Don Ellis (the guy who signed us to Epic) was long gone by then. But we weren't too worried much about that because we were excited about our latest batch of material. So we did up some demo recordings in a small studio in Austin, sent them off to our new Epic A&R gal, Bonnie Garner, and waited for her to say, "Attaboy!"

Sadly, there were no attaboys to be heard, because I guess you'd say Bonnie was underwhelmed. When word came down from on high, it was not good: "The material isn't strong enough, so we're gonna let you go." So that made us two for two on record companies—two albums, two labels, two drops. Batting a thousand, in other words (or zero). Us being the toast of Texas just was not enough for Epic Records, I guess.

Fortunately, we had friends elsewhere. One guy at Epic who always liked us was Bill Williams, the head of promotion, and he left the label before we did. He'd landed at Capitol Records, Stoney Edwards's label, and it seemed only fitting that we'd wind up there, too. And so it was that 1975 found us hooking up with suitor number three, Capitol Records. We went into Cowboy Jack Clement's studio in Nashville and reunited with Tommy

Allsup, our old friend from *Comin' Right at Ya*, to make the album that became *Texas Gold*.

We recorded the tracks on *Texas Gold* live with not too many overdubs, which was complicated because we were up to a ten-piece band by then, and we also had at least that many guest players come in for various tracks—it was truly a party in there all the time. Mr. "Okie from Muskogee" himself, Merle Haggard, was recording in Clement's other studio at the same time. Merle's band included Eldon Shamblin and Tiny Moore from Bob Wills's Texas Playboys, so there were two of our guests right there. Those guys *had* to be on the record.

Fortunately, Tommy managed to handle everything we threw at him and keep all the balls in the air, and he captured Asleep at the Wheel in all our ragged stoner-twang glory. We split vocals between Chris, Leroy, and me, with original tunes and our usual assortment of cool covers. We covered Bob Wills, of course, with "Trouble in Mind"; and also songs by the early R&B great Big Joe Turner and Toussaint McCall, an unjustly obscure soul singer from Louisiana. It came out great—our best album yet.

Ed Ward, my old friend from Antioch College, gave *Texas Gold* a very nice review in *Rolling Stone* magazine, although he did say it had "one of the worst album covers since the wane of psychedelia." But I liked that cover a lot. It was designed by an Austin artist by the name of Jack White (who later went on to become the "Official Texas State Artist" and even an honorary admiral in the Texas Navy). For years, he would make gold-leaf etchings on glass with Western-themed scenes and sell them at flea markets. Then his ship came in when the McDonald's fast-food chain bought a million bucks worth of his etchings, and they were suddenly everywhere.

Ed, thanks for the review, but I still think you were wrong about the cover.

The one bummer was that we could never come up with a decent song called "Texas Gold," which felt like a missed opportunity, but everything else about the album came up top-dead-center.

*Texas Gold* had all the songs Epic had rejected, including a tear-jerker ballad called "The Letter That Johnny Walker Read." Pun and all, the title was suggested by Chris Frayne, Commander Cody's brother. Leroy and I took his suggestion and ran with it, writing "Letter" at our practice space. We thought it would be a great duet for Dolly Parton and Porter Wagoner, so we sent a copy of our demo to Porter care of his studio. Never heard a word back, and Epic obviously didn't think much of it, either. Oh well.

So we recorded it with Chris and me doing the vocals instead of Dolly and Porter. Capitol chose it as the album's first single, and damn if it didn't turn into our biggest hit ever. It climbed all the way to number ten on the country charts, and *Texas Gold* did even better, reaching number seven on the country album charts (also still a peak for us). We even crossed over and made it into the lower reaches of the pop album charts for the first time.

The label's advertising department swung into action and took out full-page ads in the trade magazines with our picture and the declaration "ASLEEP AT THE WHEEL is on Capitol . . . AND ON THE CHARTS!" True, those ads also called *Texas Gold* our "debut album" when it was actually our third, but what the hell. And when Grammy nominations came out, *Texas Gold* picked up two—one for best duo/group vocal for the album, and another for best country instrumental for "Fat Boy Rag." Didn't win either, but the attention was nice.

Two other singles from *Texas Gold* would make the Top 40 of the country charts, "Nothin' Takes the Place of You" and "Bump, Bounce, Boogie." But "The Letter that Johnny Walker Read" was still that album's drawing card, and all these years later it remains our biggest single ever. Despite that, we rarely play it live anymore because to tell you the truth, I never much liked it. It's slow and maudlin, and there's that spoken recitation in the middle. I could never do it with a straight face even back when I had to, so I started making jokes out of it. I came up with this whole bit about Johnny Walker being drunk, coming home to his poor wife and finding her in bed with Boxcar Willie—"a hobosexual making love to his wife."

Even though people always laughed, it's probably for the best that we gave that up. But we'll still break it out on occasion.

Asleep at the Wheel would make a total of eight albums for Capitol in two stints, through the rest of the 1970s and then during a couple of years in the 1990s, which I guess makes it the label we were on the longest. Most of our Capitol albums made respectable showings on the country charts, usually selling in the neighborhood of at least 100,000 copies, and we had a few singles do okay, too. But to Capitol's unending frustration, we never topped either *Texas Gold* or "The Letter That Johnny Walker Read," and that success turned out to be kind of a mixed blessing.

Once we'd had a hit, Capitol started throwing songs at us written by people like Rupert Holmes—you know, the guy who had a number-one pop hit with "Escape (The Piña Colada Song)"—just because that's what record companies always do. To them, Asleep at the Wheel wasn't a band so much as a brand to try and jam into whatever slot seemed hot. I could have told them that all their crossover efforts would be wasted on us because, as ol' Waylon Jennings used to say, I couldn't go pop with ten firecrackers in my mouth.

The music business is all marketing and money and people believing in things whether they're real or not. With just about every label we've ever been on, what it came down to was that they wanted us to make hits, while we wanted to make history. The history I had in mind was recording two-track with the old Texas Playboys guys, straight to tape with a fourteen-piece big band playing Big Joe Turner R&B songs done up as Bob Wills–style Western swing. And they wanted us doing, well, songs about piña coladas. But there's already one Jimmy Buffett out there. Then or now, I've never seen the point in us trying to be anybody but us.

The hell of it was that I think Asleep at the Wheel *could* have had more hits, on our own terms, if everybody had just let us be our weird-ass selves and quit trying to force us into things.

The Capitol album I was proudest of was *The Wheel*, from 1977. Great record, our first with all originals and no covers. In the early '80s, Rodney Crowell would take two songs Leroy had written on that album and record them with his wife, Rosanne Cash. Her versions of both were huge country hits. "My Baby Thinks He's a Train" hit number one, and "I Wonder" got to number eight.

Okay, maybe Rosanne had a hit with "Train" and we didn't because we cut our version like a rockabilly song from 1958, with echo and slap bass. I'd rather that had been the single from "The Wheel," but Capitol put out "Let's Face Up" instead and it stiffed. Oh well. "The Wheel" still got to number 31 on the country album chart, not a bad showing.

That Robert Christgau fellow up in New York City thought enough of *The Wheel* to give us another A-minus and props for our "dumb eloquence," and the readers of *Rolling Stone* magazine voted us Best Country & Western Band. We somehow even got an award out of the Academy of Country Music—Touring Band of the Year—in 1977. Then came that Grammy, for a song off 1978's *Collision Course*.

Things seemed to be looking up. But they were about to start looking rough.

# "Framed"

EVEN THOUGH *Collision Course* won Asleep at the Wheel that first Grammy, it wasn't exactly a big seller. It had one single that charted, "Texas Me and You," but it only got up to number 75. So, yeah, we were four albums in with Capitol; not really getting beyond a certain commercial plateau, kind of spinning our wheels (har har). What next? That was when they suggested we do a live album.

Friends, I've since come to understand that proposing a live album is a record label's polite way of throwing its hands up and saying, "You're fixin' to get fired—but first let's slap together one last quickie and try to get us some of our money back." Live albums cost less to record, and they give everyone a way out while keeping that contractually obligated merry-go-round turning for one more cycle. It was obvious that Capitol thought Asleep at the Wheel's well had about run dry. So we recorded *Served Live* at the Austin Opera House; and sure enough, the label dropped us not long after putting that album out in 1979.

There was an exodus under way within the band by then, too. Leroy Preston, Floyd Domino, and Tony Garnier had all taken their leave after *Collision Course*. Leroy continued on as a solo act and is still best known as a writer of hits for others, thanks to Rosanne Cash. Floyd went off to seek his fortune in

New York, playing in the Broadway run of *The Best Little Whorehouse in Texas*. He's come back to play with Asleep at the Wheel again a lot of times over the years, and he's always welcome. But Floyd wound up spending most of his time in the backup band of somebody who used to open for us, the lead singer of a band called Ace in the Hole.

In 1978, we were playing at Gruene Hall in Texas and I was on our bus, hearing Ace in the Hole playing Texas shuffles and Western swing. They were good, and when I went in for a closer listen, the singer was even better. That was a fellow by the name of George Strait, and he took Western swing a lot higher up the charts than we ever did. George's Ace in the Hole and Asleep at the Wheel played for three hundred people at Gruene Hall that night. A few years later, we were opening for George—in stadiums, which we've done a bunch over the years. The biggest shows of all were on George's The Cowboy Rides Away Tour, especially the finale in June 2014. That one drew almost 105,000 people(!), breaking attendance records previously held by the Rolling Stones and U2. Naturally, we had two bus breakdowns getting there. But we made that gig, by God.

As for Tony, he went the journeyman route and played with everybody from rockabilly man Robert Gordon to the *Saturday Night Live* house band. Eventually, he joined Bob Dylan's Never Ending Tour band in 1989. As of this writing, the tour has yet to end, and Tony is still keeping his vigil on bass. Asleep at the Wheel has opened for Dylan some over the years, and he is a very strange cat. Brilliant, of course, but very much on his own wavelength. I've learned that the main thing is not to try and write like him, even though the hardest thing in the world is to hear a Dylan record and then *not* want to do that. The man is just a whole lot smarter than anyone else, including you and me put together.

People seem baffled at some of the things Dylan has done, like a Christmas album and a Victoria's Secret commercial and *Self Portrait*. Me, I just think back to the time when we were on tour with Bob and he walked up to me and asked, "Ray, what's a train hear with?" I said I didn't know and Bob said, "With engi-nEERS," and he giggled and walked off.

Yep, that's him: voice of a generation.

Lucky Oceans decided he'd had enough, too, and quit after *Served Live*. My childhood friend's departure left a large void in my band and my life, but I sure couldn't blame him. He'd fallen in love with a gal from Australia, and she wanted to move home. So they got married, had a kid, and off they went Down Under. Thanks to the exchange rate, Lucky was able to buy a couple of houses on the beach for around forty grand that are both worth over a million now. He's been on the radio for years down there, living in Perth and doing a world-music show with the Australian Broadcasting Corporation. Still plays pedal steel in bands, too.

After Lucky left, it was down to me and Chris O'Connell as the last of Asleep at the Wheel's original core members, although she and I were no longer a couple. Things were always stormy between us—put an Irish alcoholic together with a Jewish control-freak businessman, add copious drinking and drugging, and sparks will fly. We had finally broken up for the last time a few years earlier, which led to some mighty ugly scenes. One happened when she started dating someone else in the band, and I caught them holding hands and necking at what had been our favorite Mexican restaurant. I had channeled a lot of the bad feelings from the breakup into the songs on *The Wheel*.

Between my breakup with Chris, the band's breakup with Capitol, and the mass departures of Lucky, Leroy, Floyd, and Tony, I think most people would have considered giving up at that point. Call it a good ten-year run; we tried, oh well, so long. As brutal as the music business can be, a ten-year career is pretty damn good. You know, there's a lot of stuff I could do. I've had chances at record-company jobs, because that's a world I can function in. But even though I've got the skills, I don't want to be in that world. Why would I? I've got the life—diverse talents and the ability to create a group of people who can consistently deliver entertainment. I've got enough of a schizophrenic mind to do both art and business, but there's no turning the musician part of my mind all the way off. I always tell people that if they can do something else, they should. But the truly creative people will never stop, even with all the problems and frustrations. That's the mark.

So, no, I didn't even give quitting a second thought. Instead, we just drafted replacements and kept on keepin' on. Danny Levin was still on fiddle, so that was another link to the old days, and Cody's steel player, Bobby Black, had joined us. We even added another girl singer, Maryann Price.

By 1980, I was twenty-nine years old and dating an eighteen-year-old beauty by the name of KK (don't judge). My roommate in Austin was Vince McGarry, the Philadelphia deejay I'd grown up listening to, who had become Asleep at the Wheel's recording engineer (later, he would also marry Chris O'Connell). And I had gotten us under contract to yet another big record company.

MCA Records was the latest label to take a shot at making Asleep at the Wheel a household name. Music Company of America. Sounded pretty all-powerful. But a few years earlier, Lynyrd Skynyrd had put out a song called "Workin' for MCA" that made it sound like indentured servitude, which should have been a warning. MCA wound up being about the most dispiriting label experience we ever had, starting with the directive from the guy who signed us. That was Jim Foglesong, and he told us, "Make a record with little or no Western swing or country music." I guess trying to get us to make a rock record was his brilliant crossover strategy.

If that's really what Foglesong wanted, well, letting me be the producer was his first mistake. I'd let him find that out soon enough. First, however, I had to find a new drummer. Two weeks before Asleep at the Wheel was to start recording, our drummer, Fran Christina, quit to go play for another band, Jimmie Vaughan's Fabulous Thunderbirds, which I used to jam with at Antone's every week. But after I got over being pissed off about the timing, I couldn't really hold that against him. Jimmie's a nut, but the Thunderbirds were great, and things worked out nicely for them a few years later when they had a big hit with "Tuff Enuff." I still had to replace Fran, though, so I got Billy Estes from Tulsa, a black man and a helluva funk player. But I had to teach him how to swing.

MCA rented us three apartments off East Riverside Drive in Austin, which we dubbed "Casa Del Amor." All of us lived there while we weren't on the road, which made it easier for us to spend twelve hours a day in the studio during recording periods. That made for a pretty crazy schedule, but it was their money. We had a $100,000 budget, a lot of money for back then. We did some cool things with it, like an homage to Doc Pomus—one of the rock era's great songwriters and storytellers, the pen behind hits for the Drifters and Elvis. We called it "Lonely Avenue Revisited," a nod to Ray Charles's "Lonely Avenue," and got Bonnie Raitt to sing on the chorus when she was in town. Also did Tony Johnson's "Midnight in Memphis," which Bette Midler had some success with later; and, just to give MCA a middle finger over Foglesong's "no country" order, Loretta Lynn's "You Wanna Give Me a Lift." Take that.

We called the album *Framed*, which seemed appropriate. And while we were pleased with it, MCA was not, and so it was doomed. Technically, *Framed* did "cross over," becoming the only Asleep at the Wheel album that ever made the pop charts but not the country charts. Unfortunately, its pop-chart peak was number 191. And so MCA returned that middle finger and dropped us.

We would spend the next five years with no label.

The early 1980s were a dark, dark time for Asleep at the Wheel, kind of the "Long March" period of our history. We were in the wilderness with no label, which meant no records, which meant no advances or radio airplay. The only way for us to make any money was to get out and play shows, and so we did, even though the lack of airplay made it an uphill climb. We were still a decent live draw, thank God. But we really were just hanging on.

The lineup turned into more of a revolving door than ever, almost too many people coming and going to keep up with. That was when the band became Ray Benson and Asleep at the Wheel, because I was the only constant throughout. Given how hard it was to keep going, I'm proud of the standard we maintained. Everybody who's ever been in Asleep at the Wheel is a great player, which is one big reason why we're still at it going on five decades later.

Despite the band's difficulties, my personal life took a major turn for the better when I met Diane Carr and we fell madly in love. I'd had girlfriends—Chris, KK, lots of others—but I knew from the get-go that this was serious, and I was determined not to screw it up. Diane was very beautiful, and smart; worked as a nurse, which pointed toward a nurturing nature. I was thirty years old and ready to start a family, and I pegged her as the one I wanted to do it with. Diane had some hesitation about that. But as I mentioned before, I can be very persuasive.

So we married in 1981. Asleep at the Wheel was more than ten years old and had had a Top 10 hit and won a Grammy Award, so we were a brand name with some value, but the lineup was ever thinning as our debts ballooned into six figures. My old car barely ran, and I had no health insurance. It looked pretty hopeless. But my solution was the same as always, to just keep working—to go until I couldn't go anymore, or until nobody showed up.

It helped that I had cultivated relationships with some bankers by then. Our balance sheet would have looked terrible to somebody who didn't know us, but we've always paid our bills and bankers know us as a legitimate business entity. True, borrowing money just meant more debt, but I kept the balancing act going for one reason that outweighed everything else: I loved what I was doing. Still do. It would have been nice to figure out how to get rich at it, but money's never been my priority.

Diane gradually started helping out with the band, becoming something like a co-manager with me. And in November 1983, our first son, Sam, was born (both our kids would be born in November, because the band tends to be home a lot during the month of February). I was thrilled. Still working my ass off, of course, and robbing Peter to pay Paul and keep this circus going. But with a little help from my dad, we did manage to scrape together just enough cash to put a down payment on a quite frankly crappy little one-bedroom house on Lake Travis, which had a sale price of $18,500 (a sum that might get you one square foot of that lot nowadays, Austin real estate prices being what they are). The place was priced to move because it had been a stash house for dope dealers.

## Deadly Sins

SPEAKING OF DOPE, I decided that becoming a father was also the right time for me to quit cocaine once and for all. Don't get me wrong—it was something I used to enjoy and it didn't ruin or take over my life. I'm not sure anybody is ever in control of their cocaine habit, but I was probably as close as you can get. Still, cocaine is a drug that creates an attitude of omnipotence. It also contributed to me making a great many stupid decisions, and saying and doing lots of things I regret. Besides which, for someone with ADD, a drug that speeds your mind up is counterproductive—which is why I gave up cocaine and don't miss it, but still smoke weed.

I certainly saw the evil parts of cocaine. But one of the few positive things about it was that it encouraged the bohemian nightlife lifestyle rooted in the jazz, blues, and rock 'n' roll history books. The buzzwords back then were "living on the edge" and "life in the fast lane," and cocaine was a big part of that. I'd actually rather deal with cokeheads than alcoholics because what I've seen of alcoholism is even worse. The alcoholic's vortex can really suck you in. Junkies, too, it's the same; the only difference is alcohol is legal. With either one, there's no control. So I'll just smoke my pot, thank you.

Ultimately, what it finally came down to was that we enjoyed pot more than coke. Willie Nelson was always ahead of his time, and he's the first one I knew who made the rule "If you're wired, you're fired." He was seeing the destruction and decadence of cocaine, and the awful things it could do. And once Sam was born, I decided I didn't want to be like the cokehead dads I saw.

Pot, however, was something else entirely, and I still smoke it to this day. I'm working on getting it legalized, and the tide does seem to be turning. But I thought the same thing when Jimmy Carter was elected president in 1976. Ironically, we once got booked to play a show in Kerrville, Texas, sponsored by D.A.R.E. (Drug Abuse Resistance Education). A benefit for drug dogs, of all things. We told them we had to keep our bus parked way far away from the stage and their drug-sniffing dogs because we had a refrigerator on board, the motor had to run, it made fumes, and I couldn't sing if there were fumes. So the bus and our pot fumes were far removed from everybody, and that was just as well.

I've gotten arrested a time or two, but somehow never charged or detained because someone up there looks after fools. In 1970 in Winchester, Virginia—Patsy Cline's birthplace—I was coming back from seeing New Riders of the Purple Sage and got caught speeding. I was high, of course, so they threw me in the drunk tank until my friends brought bail. There were two other drunks in there, one crying about his life being ruined and the other hollering, "Get me outta here, I ain't sharing no cell with no long-haired lesbian."

Otherwise, I've been luckier than I deserve to be. My favorite quote from Branch Rickey, the Dodgers manager who integrated baseball with Jackie Robinson, is this: "Luck is the residue of design." That's brilliant. Think, design and plan it, then let luck take over. Some people from the band, who shall remain nameless, were so negative, and things always seemed to work out that way. Say something good won't happen and it probably won't. I take the other tack: "*Of course* it's gonna happen and be great. The glass is always half full, and I'll drink the rest." The eternal optimist, that's me. With or without drugs, I'm the guy who wakes up every day thinking (or at least hoping) that something great is about to happen.

During my druggie days in the '70s, one of the great things that happened was making the acquaintance of a hotshot young blues guitarist in Austin. Stevie Vaughan. This was before he added "Ray" in the middle of his name and established himself as one of the most epic guitar players of the twentieth century. Back then, he was still known as kid brother to Jimmie Vaughan of the Fabulous Thunderbirds, and he was still very much in his big brother's shadow. But he was great from the get-go. He played with Paul Ray and the Cobras, the hottest blues band in town, and then with Lou Ann Barton in Triple Threat.

Stevie Ray was living in a nine-hundred-square-foot house on a dirt road behind the Safeway in South Austin and doing way too much speed. Having been there and done that, I tried to talk some sense into him about speed. But I wasn't exactly above reproach when it came to drugs myself, and there really wasn't a thing I could say when he got into coke—even though I tried to talk him down from the edge of that cliff after I quit cocaine in 1983. He had to find his way back from that on his own, and he struggled with substance abuse for years before finally quitting everything in the mid-1980s. The good part was that he stayed clean for the rest of his life. The bad part, as you know, was that the rest of Stevie Ray's life wasn't very long. He died in a helicopter crash after a show in 1990, leaving so much undone that it still hurts to think about it.

He lived only to the age of thirty-five, but Stevie Ray left behind an amazing body of work and incredible memories for all of us who were lucky enough to see him play. In the early 1980s, I hooked him up with our booking agent, Alex Hodge, who became his manager and guided him to the top. Now, I do things for people all the time and they never remember. Stevie Ray, he never forgot. We were playing a fair once, Asleep at the

Wheel on a side stage with the Judds and Stevie Ray over on the main stage. He came over, sat in the front row, and watched our entire set. People don't remember how supportive he always was, even after he hit it big. In my experience, he was always a kind person and a nice man.

Once Stevie Ray caught on with the masses, his rocket ride was pretty incredible to watch. Outside of Austin, the first that most people heard of Stevie Ray was on David Bowie's 1983 album *Let's Dance*. Bowie's a legend and his album sold millions and was all over MTV, but Stevie Ray was unimpressed.

"Aw, I just played Albert King licks all over his shit," he said when I asked him about it, and he made a little face.

Stevie Ray's own album *Texas Flood* came out that same year, and then everybody knew he was a lot more than an Albert King imitator. After he'd broken through, I remember seeing him pull out Jimi Hendrix's "Voodoo Chile" at the Paramount Theatre in Austin. All the blues purists were just aghast, but they couldn't see how far Stevie Ray had already gone past them. The rest of us were just amazed.

Stoned or straight, Stevie Ray was always an astonishing player to watch, even if he could be hard to take for anybody onstage with him. I went to see him play this all-star thing before he sobered up and he was coked out, twitching, all over the place and not leaving a bit of room for anyone else. Dr. John, a man who knows a thing or two about mind-altering substances himself, was onstage too, and he could tell what was happening. He called it to a halt and announced, "What we *need* here is some, uh, *dynamicals*."

Everybody who ever jammed with Stevie Ray had a similar experience, but it wasn't just the drugs talking. I remember one late-night jam in this old union hall near where he lived. When you're jamming like that, you play until you relinquish the solo spot; go until you run out of ideas and then let somebody else jump in. Stevie Ray, however, just would not let up. He kept on playing and playing and playing, to the point where everybody else got fed up. Nobody got mad, exactly, but we were all a little irritated because he was hogging the jam.

The line you always heard about the Vaughan brothers was that Jimmie played only some of what he knew because he's a great, understated player, while Stevie Ray played every last thing he knew every time. Which was true, and after he died, I thought back to that jam session. Somewhere deep down, it almost seemed like Stevie Ray knew he would not be here for long. So he put it all out there and never held back a thing. Playing guitar was a full-body experience for him. I went to his house once and found him practicing making faces like B. B. King, getting his whole body into it.

He never stopped, even when he was asleep. His wife, Lenny, has talked about waking up at night beside Stevie Ray and seeing that he was moving his hands—playing guitar in his sleep. Sleep guitar. She'd just watch, and listen. I bet it was worth hearing.

I miss him.

Once I was cocaine-free, I assessed my situation. I was a father, plus the leader and manager of a band trying to make a living playing a retro style of music that had been out of fashion for thirty years. And while there's no pot of gold at the end of the Western swing rainbow, as Vince Gill likes to say, I did find the next best thing: Lake Tahoe, a place I'd first visited with my family when I was seven years old. It hadn't gotten any more wholesome since then, but that was okay.

Asleep at the Wheel had first started playing Harrah's Casino at Lake Tahoe a few years earlier, and it became one of our most reliable regular plays during the fallow '80s. They'd book a lot of first-rate acts, like B. B. King, Fats Domino, Fifth Dimension, Willie and Merle, and some oddball ones, too, like circus acts on unicycles and Joe Savage, this guy who wore a fur jockstrap, had a rock cover band, and did a lot of pyro. And us, speaking of circus-type acts. We opened for Frank Sinatra Jr. once. Got to rub elbows with Sammy Davis Jr., too, which was a trip. I was looking around for the rest of the Rat Pack. They were probably there somewhere.

Harrah's booker was Stu Carnall, and he would put us into "The Cabaret," as it was called. Stu was a stereotypical old show-biz guy who managed Johnny Cash at one point, and he was Bob Wills's agent in the 1950s. He told me the real stories about Bob, like taking him to whorehouses in Fresno between shows. Bob could draw crowds in the thousands in Oakland, where we used to live, because of the shipyards there. Rednecks are everywhere, as I've come to discover.

I paid off many a debt thanks to Stu booking us into Harrah's, and I also learned how to put together a very tight, musical, and entertaining hour-long set. It's all about pacing. We'd do two one-hour shows every weeknight, then three a night on the week-ends. Some might find that grueling, but it was nothing compared to the grind we used to endure backing up Stoney Edwards and everyone else in the early '70s. It felt just like going to the gym.

Late nights at Harrah's could be adventuresome, because that last set might not start until well after two a.m. It was about that late one night when we were behind the curtain listening to the announcer: "Ladies and gentlemen, Harrah's Lake Tahoe is proud to present Grammy-winning Western swing band Asleep at the Wheel!" Curtain went up and the "crowd" consisted of one guy—yes, one, uno, eins—who was very drunk, clapping and hollering. I was singing "Miles and Miles of Texas" and that guy was still yelling, "YAY!" He did not let up the entire hour. But by the end of that set, he was no longer alone because four people were there. Success!

We did manage to screw up and get fired at Harrah's, more than once, usually for smoking dope. But our most memorable Tahoe termination was when Maryann was singing "I'm an Old Cowhand from the Rio Grande," which has the line "My legs ain't bowed and my cheeks ain't tanned." She'd hike her skirt up at that line, and on this particular night she wasn't wearing no panties. There was a collective gasp from everyone in the room, including me. I couldn't tell if she'd meant to do it or not. Anyway, we were fired for her "indiscretion." Oh well. It wasn't long before they forgave us and booked Asleep at the Wheel again.

You could say the deadly sins were doing right by Asleep at the Wheel, because our other big gravy train back then was actually a beer train, pulled by a team of Clydesdale horses. It started about 1981, when our then-manager got together all our press clippings from the past two years of shows in bars, highlighted every reference to "beer-drinking crowd" and sent it off to Budweiser's advertising agency. It was a brilliant pitch, and it worked. Budweiser sponsored us, paid to have our bus painted, and gave us things like Budweiser Hawaiian shirts and neon to put onstage.

Even better, they hired us to do advertising jingles. Whether you knew it or not, you heard a lot of me on your TV if you were watching sports at all during the '80s. A deep baritone voice saying, "For all you do, this Bud's for you"—remember that? Well, that was me, and it ran for years. The residuals from that and other spots I sang and produced kept us above water for most of the decade.

A few years later, I was doing some production work with country acts like Ricky Van Shelton and Sweethearts of the Rodeo, and an amazing young country singer from Canada named k.d. lang. I got them all to record songs about beer in their style for Budweiser commercials, which worked out great; k.d. especially loved that because she wasn't identified, and she didn't have to hear it because she was living in Canada. Plus she made ten grand, and residuals. What's not to like?

Someone else I got in on the Budweiser windfall was Vince Gill, who was then married to Janis Oliver from Sweethearts of the Rodeo (this was before he married Amy Grant). Can't recollect the first time Vince and I met—first time I remember was at the Playboy Mansion in the '70s, when Sweethearts of the Rodeo were playing some sort of charity show. Vince was in a group called Sundance then, a few years before joining Pure Prairie League. Then he joined Rodney Crowell's band the Notorious Cherry Bombs, and it was obvious that he was one of the sweetest guitar players and harmony singers on earth.

Vince and I bonded over music, guitars, and golf. You know, guitar guys are guitar guys, and he's a guy with a million-dollar collection who plays 'em all. Back then, though, his lifestyle was a little more modest. I asked Vince once if he wanted to play on a Budweiser spot, and he said he couldn't because he had to babysit.

"Vince," I said, "I'll pay you three hundred bucks. You can hire a babysitter for less than that."

He did the spot and got paid.

# Write Your Own Song

AS THE '80S WORE ON, survival was the goal. When we weren't on the road, I'd go into the office, pick up my address book, and start calling people, trying to get something going, anything going. Diane was busy raising Sam, so we really had no manager except for me. I've been told that the only reason Asleep at the Wheel has survived for so long is because I just won't take no for an answer, but I sure did get that answer a lot back then.

Onstage, we continued giving the people what they wanted. And what the people wanted out of Asleep at the Wheel was the old Bob Wills–style Western swing and boogie-woogie, which became more and more the heart of the act. We still went over great in Texas, Tulsa, and places like the Cotillion Ballroom in Wichita, Kansas. Even New York City, where we were sort of a novelty and people showed up saying Asleep at the Wheel was their favorite band without even knowing what we really did; at least they paid to get in. But there were also nights in places like Winchester, Virginia (same town where I'd been thrown in the drunk tank back in 1970), where the only person who showed up was Chris O'Connell's mother. We'd have stretches of one terrible gig after another.

It's during the tough times that you figure out if something like life in a touring band really is your thing, and it's definitely mine—my mission in life, you might say. Great fun, in between the heartbreak. Every time I get onstage, I love watching people dance, and there have been plenty of nights when that had to be enough. Nights when we'd have to figure out how to rig the bus to get to the gig and ride for hours with no heat, wondering if freezing to death was really worth it for $250 a week.

For a lot of folks, that answer became no. Chris O'Connell finally came to the end of the line in 1986, ending a tumultuous decade and a half. She was the last of the original core besides me to still be there, but it was time. When she quit, Chris was married, pregnant, and due to become a mother in a few months. Fifteen years, many of them spent as the only woman in a band of crazy dudes, had been enough.

I must have fired and rehired Chris at least a dozen times over the years, especially after Maryann joined. Those two were partners in a lot of crime. I remember one particularly bad airport scene where they were drinking martinis, breaking shit up, and racing a stolen cart around the wrong terminal; if they hadn't held the flight for us, we would've missed it. We'd have horrible fights where I'd tell Chris she needed to get the hell off my bandstand, and she'd say fine. Then we'd really start on each other, and it always seemed to end with a whole round of, "Okay, just get on the bus," "No! You just fired me," and so on. And on and on and on.

As time went by, I became one of many people who were haranguing Chris to get help. She finally did, and I paid for her to spend a month at a substance-abuse treatment clinic. She did the time, did the work, and did her last few years in the band sober, which helped a lot. But sparks still flew on occasion up until the end. Dave Sanger joined the band as drummer toward the end of Chris's time, and there were times when I'd be yelling at him to speed up the tempo while Chris was yelling for him to slow down.

Somehow, we all managed, and Chris and I parted on friendly terms. I would not trade her time in Asleep at the Wheel for anything, but I consider it equal parts accomplishment and miracle that neither of us killed the other.

You could probably say something similar about Junior Brown, even though he was Asleep at the Wheel's steel player for only about four months. A great talent and one of many wonderful steel players we've had over the years, including Lucky and Eddie Rivers and the great Cindy Cashdollar. I like Junior, but he and I just never seemed to get along. Junior was in the Wheel in the mid-'80s, before he'd come up with his trademark "guit-steel," so he'd go back and forth between pedal and lap steel guitars onstage. Sometimes that was a problem.

Junior's unplanned and unannounced departure from Asleep at the Wheel happened at a show at Southfork Ranch in Texas, where the TV series *Dallas* was filmed. It was this thing where they taught Western dance while we played. "We're gonna do a Texas two-step now," I announced, "and Junior's gonna kick it off." Everybody was poised and ready to go, band and dancers—except for Junior, who seemed to be moving in slow motion. After what felt like ten minutes of fumbling around, he still wasn't ready.

"Ol' Junior's having some problems with his steel guitar," I said. "Larry, kick it off."

So we finished the set a bit later and were on our break when someone came running up to tell me Junior was leaving. I climbed up onstage to take a look and sure enough, he was on a golf cart with his amp and steel, going down that long Southfork driveway. In forty-five years, that's still the weirdest way I've ever had anybody quit.

That was on a Thursday, and I didn't hear from Junior until the following Monday, when he came into the office to demand his paycheck. "Junior," I said, "you not only quit in the middle of the week, you quit in the middle of a gig."

I refused to pay him.

If gambling casinos and beer commercials got us through the first half of the '80s, it was chicken tenders that got us back to dealing with record labels. In the mid-'80s, John Tyson from the Arkansas-based chicken-empire family of the same name decided he wanted to start a record label. So he formed one called Marble Records and hired a couple of guys who used to work for CBS Records to run it.

Marble's first move was to sign Dave Mason, formerly of Steve Winwood's supergroup Traffic; they had a line on Mason because he used to record for CBS. Then they signed us. Asleep at the Wheel was a known quantity because Tyson Foods used to hire us to play their parties, and we played a lot of them. Met Bill Clinton at one, too, when he was still governor of Arkansas and thinking about running for president. I remember us being asked to take a break so that they could have a chicken-plucking contest, where all these high rollers took off their jackets, rolled up their sleeves, and started stripping off feathers. Bill was in there plucking away, too.

Anyway, finally rejoining the ranks of the signed gave us an excuse to get some more material together. Willie Nelson let us use his studio, and it went well. Things were going along just fine until somebody at Tyson apparently figured out that a record company was going to be a money pit they couldn't afford. Tyson unceremoniously pulled the plug, and Marble Records went out of business, never having released an album.

Still, we managed to put our record out on small independent labels in Canada and England. Asleep at the Wheel's first new album in five long years was called *Pasture Prime*, with songs by John Hiatt (still largely unknown at that point) and, of course, our man Bob Wills. Texas Playboys fiddler Johnny Gimble was playing with us at that point, and having him on an Asleep at the Wheel record was a thrill for us.

*Pasture Prime* also had a song written by our buddy Willie Nelson, and he and I did it as a duet. "Write Your Own Song" detailed every musician's frustrations with how label people seem to think it's so easy to write hits: "If you think it is, Mr. Music Executive / Why don't you write your own songs?" To my surprise, that didn't keep an American label from picking it up for the U.S. market. Jimmy Bowen, one of the few label guys out there with an actual clue, was at our former label MCA Records then. He didn't sign us, but he bought the rights to our album, retitled it simply *Asleep at the Wheel*, and put out a shortened version on MCA's country imprint Dot Records in 1985.

As we moved on into 1986, things were picking up in my world and getting better than they'd been in quite a while. My second son, Aaron, was born that year, so now Diane had two little boys to manage. Tending to Sam and Aaron kept her plenty busy. Meanwhile, I tended to business.

*Pasture Prime/Asleep at the Wheel* didn't do much at the cash register, but it did get us back on the radar at an opportune moment. The mid-'80s was when Nashville started giving cool left-of-center acts a shot. Lyle Lovett, Steve Earle, and Dwight Yoakam all put out major-label debut albums in 1986, with k.d. lang, Lucinda Williams, Nanci Griffith, and more right behind them.

Asleep at the Wheel didn't sound a thing like any of them, of course, but change was in the air. It seemed like things were loosening up enough that maybe, just maybe, we could get another shot, too. Time for us to make our move, so we did.

Our old bass player Spencer Starnes had a recording studio set up in a mobile home in Austin, and I traded him three microphones for enough studio time for us to cut three songs. Then we sent those tracks off to CBS Records, which at that time was in the shitter after signing all these pop acts that did nothing. Rick Blackburn was the guy in charge there, and he was in the market for new acts. Right around the same time, he signed Rodney Crowell, the O'Kanes, Rattlesnake Annie, and us. Asleep at the Wheel was back on the CBS imprint Epic Records, a dozen years after they'd dropped us, but who's keeping track? Me, I guess.

Shortly after signing our Epic deal, we were on the road coming through Nashville, where we pulled into Shoney's Inn and saw Merle Haggard's touring bus. So we went on in there to socialize and smoke a joint. Yes, "We don't smoke marijuana in Muskogee" might be the first line of Merle Haggard's most famous song, but I'm here to tell you I have witnessed otherwise. So we all got pleasantly buzzed, and after a while Merle got sort of a mischievous look on his face.

"Hey," he said with a gleam in his eye, "how about you come with me to kick a little ass over at the record company?"

Sure, I said, I'm always up for that. So off Merle and I went to the CBS Records offices on Music Row, and we went into Rick Blackburn's office. Larry Hamby, the head of A&R, was there, too. We exchanged pleasantries for a bit, and then Merle inquired about his latest advance, the size of which he found wanting. Near as I can recall decades later, here's how the conversation went down.

"How come," Merle asked, "you only gave me five hundred thousand dollars and not the million I wanted?"

"Because," Blackburn said, "your last album didn't sell shit."

That was *Kern River*, which had come out in 1985 and probably sold a few hundred thousand copies. Not bad numbers unless you compare it to the *Pancho & Lefty* album he'd done with Willie a few years earlier—that one sold well over a million.

"*Kern River* didn't sell shit because you didn't promote it," Merle said.

"Well, Merle, it didn't sell because the songs were lousy," Blackburn said, and then Merle got mad. Really, really mad.

"And who the *fuck* are you to tell me that?" Merle said. "When's the last time *you* wrote a song?"

It was like watching "Write Your Own Song" come to life. Blackburn said he didn't write songs, but he'd sold a few. That didn't impress Merle, and they continued going back and forth, growing more and more heated.

At this point, I should mention that Blackburn had spina bifida. That would have taken the edge off of most people. But Merle could not have cared less, and he didn't hold back.

"Goddammit," he finally screamed, "I'll kick your fucking crippled ass with one arm tied behind my fucking back!"

Now that's the Okie from Muskogee I remember. Yes, another great moment in politically incorrect music history. I've seen a few.

# *The Zen of Willie*

ASLEEP AT THE WHEEL didn't get no million bucks out of CBS, either, or even the half million Merle Haggard got. We were had for the bargain-basement price of $50,000. That's how much Rick Blackburn gave us to do another seven songs to go with the three we'd already recorded, which would be our next album.

We went back to that mobile-home studio and got to work. CBS sent their head of A&R down to check up on us at one point, which made me nervous because we were working in the sort of weird setup that tends to freak out major labels. I asked if the guy was gonna nark on us about recording in a mobile home.

"Naw," he said. "Sounds fine."

Whew. But for once, I didn't need to worry, because it *did* sound fine. And this time the world would agree.

We called the album *10*, because it was our tenth record, and it came out in 1987. *10* was the record that brought Asleep at the Wheel all the way back, starting with the first single, "Way Down Texas Way"—a Billy Joe Shaver tune that Willie's nephew Fred Fletcher suggested we do. We scraped together five grand and made a video with couples two-stepping at the Broken Spoke in Austin, plus shots of us, Willie Nelson, George Strait, Bob Wills, Gene Autry, Hank Williams, Merle Travis, and even Austin's newest hit-makers the Fabulous Thunderbirds (hey, Fran!).

"Way Down Texas Way" made the country Top 40. Considering how long Asleep at the Wheel had been absent from the charts, that was a cool drink of water in the desert, and it was just one of four country chart hits we had on *10*. But the album's biggest money shot was the second single, "House of Blue Lights," which I still think is the culmination of everything good about Asleep at the Wheel—contemporary but based on an old song from the 1940s, swing but not retro, and perfectly timed. It was a song that Bob Brown, manager of our old Bay Area pal Huey Lewis, suggested we ought to do, and he was right. "House of Blue Lights" was a hit, getting to number 17 on the country charts. It's still our second-biggest hit ever.

*10* did one notch better than "House of Blue Lights," reaching number 16 on the country album charts. I wrote one of the hits, "Boogie Back to Texas," and we covered a Guy Clark song because us Texans have to stick together. As thanks for Bob Brown's turning us on to "House of Blue Lights," we also covered Huey Lewis and the News' 1983 megahit "I Want a New Drug" as a Western swing tune. Even got Pete Anderson, Dwight Yoakam's guitarist, to play on that track.

As originally planned by the producer (me), our friend Willie Nelson was supposed to be on *10*, too. We recorded "House of Blue Lights" with a vocal cameo from Willie, but then Rick Blackburn stepped in and forced us to take Willie off of it—which he had the power to do, since Willie also recorded for CBS. Another of Willie's own singles was about to come out, and Blackburn didn't want him competing with himself. And since "House of Blue Lights" did fine without Willie, I have to admit it was the right call (albeit for the wrong reasons).

Anyway, we had our hit, even if Blackburn managed to piss Willie off just as much as he'd pissed Merle off. That might be the maddest I've ever seen either of them.

For those of you who can't imagine Willie Nelson ever getting mad, it does happen. Not often, though, because he's usually way too Zen for that. Of the many things he's a master of, laughing things off might be at the top of the list. It's a useful skill, one I wish I was better at myself.

Willie is a Pied Piper, and where he goes many follow. Some flourish, but most fall short. It's not for the faint of heart. Following Willie is an incredible trip that involves joy, fear, danger, and lessons learned. He's full of wisdom and advice, even though there are a lot of things that work for Willie and no one else.

He's also as loyal a friend as you could hope for. There was a Country Music Association anniversary show that Asleep at the Wheel and Willie were both booked on. But it was during the '80s, right around the time First Lady Nancy Reagan had started her big "Just Say No" war on drugs. The producer came to us and said, "We have to cut you from the show because Mrs. Reagan is coming on to do an anti-drug message." So I went to Willie's bus and told him and Kris Kristofferson that we were off the show and going back to Austin. They asked why and I told them.

"Then fuck 'em," Willie said. "We won't play either."

Willie's roadie went and told the producer. Funny thing, we were suddenly back on the show. That wasn't the first or last favor he's ever done for me. During our down period in the early '80s, Willie gave us $10,000 as an advance on a record deal that was in the works. The deal fell through, and of course the money was spent by then. But Willie just laughed it off—and never asked for it back. That's just one of many debts I owe him.

But we watch each other's backs, Willie and I. Like the time in 1991 when I was hired to set up a Texas music festival at the Kennedy Center in Washington, D.C. I booked the Fabulous Thunderbirds, Bobby Bland, Nanci Griffith, and (of course) Asleep at the Wheel and Willie. The first Iraq War had just begun, and Willie had put out an antiwar song that outraged Robert Mosbacher, President George H. W. Bush's commerce secretary—who demanded that we dis-invite Willie.

"I will *not* dis-invite Willie Nelson," I told him. "And if *you* try to dis-invite him, I will resign, refuse to play the festival, ask everyone else to do the same, and go to the press."

He backed off.

I had my first introduction to Willie's World at age ten with my old pink transistor radio, when I heard Patsy Cline singing "Crazy" late one night. That was heavy, even for a kid. By the time Willie and I actually met, ten years later, I knew he was the writer behind those words. It was during our time backing up Stoney Edwards and Friends on one of those death-march package tours the agents were so fond of. Five dates, shady promoter. Willie was supposed to play with us on the last date, but as soon as he showed up he figured out that nobody was getting paid. So he left. Fools that we were, we played. Got played, too, because we didn't get paid. That was the first lesson Willie taught me, and I've been learning from him ever since.

I tried to reciprocate once when we were playing golf, by showing him the "right" way to swing a club. He appreciated the advice but declined to follow any way but his own.

"Ya know," he said, "if there's a right way to do something, I'll try the wrong way first. Hell, when I did things 'their way,' nothing happened. It wasn't until I started doing things my way that it started working for me."

True enough. It was only after he got sick of Nashville politics, started ignoring the business types' conventional wisdom, and went home to Texas that Willie Nelson became Willie. You can tell the true icons because they're the ones who don't need more than one name. And if you don't think Willie knows exactly what he's doing at all times, you're wrong.

One time, this guy was taking pictures and giving Willie instructions, telling him where to turn his head. Finally, Willie looks at the guy and says, "I've got an idea. How about I be Willie Nelson, and you be the photographer? Now take the picture."

Picture turned out fine.

Willie did his first big Fourth of July picnic in Dripping Springs, Texas, in 1973. Asleep at the Wheel didn't get to play it until the following year, when it was over in Bryan. I remember that day was just broiling hot. At one point during the heat of the afternoon, a huge column of smoke arose out in the fields that had been turned into parking lots. A car's overheated exhaust had set fire to the grass and caused an inferno. Turned out that car belonged to Robert Earl Keen, who went on to a great singer-songwriter career of his own and would appear on one of our Bob Wills tribute albums (years later, he used a picture of his car going up in flames at Willie's 1974 picnic as cover art for an album).

Alas, our ratty old Scenicruiser bus's generator was dead as a doornail. That meant no traveling at night for us, so we had to leave well before dark. But we had a great time. Met Guy Clark and Leon Russell, two of my idols. And hanging out with Willie in his element is always fun, watching how he can work a crowd.

I've never been big-time, just sort of medium-time, which is a nice way to be. I get recognized just enough where people take pictures and say nice things (and sometimes stupid things, but what the hell). Met a guy once who had my face tattooed on his shoulder, which he wanted me to sign so he could turn that into a tattoo, too. That was weird, but a one-time thing for me. Willie encounters similar monuments to himself just about every day, and I've never seen him be anything but unfailingly kind and gracious about it.

He always seems to get back what he puts out, too, which is humor and grace. I saw him outside his bus signing autographs once where a lady came up and handed him something to sign.

"Whose name would you like me to put on this?" he asked.

"Well," she said, "I'd like you to sign yours."

Just walking around with Willie in public is an amazing experience, the way people are drawn to him. Most people in his position would put the deflector shields up, but not Willie. I've been playing golf with him where somebody the next fairway over says, "That's Willie Nelson." And he'll stop the cart, walk all the way over, and stick his hand out: "Hi, nice to meet you." The next time I see Willie turn down anybody for anything will be the first. That's why he has people whose job is to save Willie from himself by keeping him from doing stuff, because he'll say "yes" to everybody—especially a friend with a joint, and I admit I'm not above asking that way myself.

One of Willie's protectors is his longtime drummer Paul English, who is almost as much of a character as Willie himself (and also the subject of a song Willie wrote chronicling some of their misadventures, "Me and Paul"). In 1977, Asleep at the Wheel was on a tour with Willie and Firefall, who were both huge. In a typical example of Willie's the-more-the-merrier side, at the last minute he added Jerry Jeff Walker to the bill at this four-thousand-seat auditorium in El Paso. We were low act on the totem pole, so our set got cut from forty-five minutes to twenty-five.

Having our set time shortened was actually okay, because I was going through a rough stretch. I was on crutches from being crushed between two bumpers when I tried to jump-start my car and my neighbor's car's brakes failed. So I was soldiering on as best I could. But that night may have been the best we played all tour. Everything was grooving along and going great as we went into our big closer, "Choo Choo Ch'Boogie." We were at twenty-seven minutes, so yeah, a little over our allotted time. But everybody in the crowd was going crazy—until they turned on the lights, and it was like all the air just went out of the building. We ground to a halt, and hardly anybody even clapped afterward.

I was furious and also heavily drugged up. As best I could on my crutches, I went rushing up to the stage manager and began screaming, and he screamed right back at me. So there we were, carrying on with this bad scene in full view of four thousand people. Paul came up behind me.

"Need this?" he asked, and handed me something. I took it without even knowing what it was, then looked down and saw that Paul had given me the .22 pistol he always carried in his boot. I said no thank you, handed it back to Paul, and continued screaming.

Willie, I'm sure, would have handled it better.

In addition to playing together a ton, Willie and I have also recorded together a good bit over the years. There was "Write

Your Own Song," of course, and he's been on all three of Asleep at the Wheel's Bob Wills tribute records. And one of these days, maybe I'll try to resurrect the version of "House of Blue Lights" with him on it—the one Rick Blackburn nixed.

Willie and Asleep at the Wheel did a whole album together, too, a project set in motion by the late Jerry Wexler. Wexler was one of the legendary greats of the music business. He produced a lot of R&B classics for Atlantic Records: Wilson Pickett, Aretha Franklin, the Drifters, Ray Charles. But he and I had a checkered history. We first met during the early days of Asleep at the Wheel, when we had some buzz. Atlantic was one of the labels that paid for us to do a demo, and their reaction was, "Group's okay but they need a new guitar player." Since I was the guitar player, that was that.

Then in the early 1980s, he and I had an ugly knock-down, drag-out over Austin blues singer Lou Ann Barton, who asked me to negotiate for her. Wexler wanted to go spend a bunch of money recording her in Muscle Shoals, when she had already made great recordings in Austin with the Fabulous Thunderbirds. The argument got pretty heated, and Wexler won because he had the money to spend. Oh well, I still think it was the wrong decision.

Years later, however, Wexler and I became good friends through our mutual affection for Bob Wills. Us Western swing fans, we just can't stay mad at each other for too long. He came to a few Asleep at the Wheel shows and we had some lovely evenings together, just shootin' the shit about old records. Before Jerry died in 2008, he was getting rid of his records and he sent me a stack of Western swing albums. It was a touching gesture, but he had an ulterior motive. He called Willie's manager and said he wanted Asleep at the Wheel and Willie to do a Western swing album together, doing songs he'd marked with "WN" on the records he sent me. He'd flagged about forty songs, so I picked a dozen and we made 2009's *Willie and the Wheel*. Wexler got to hear seven of the final mixes before he died, and we credited him as the album's executive producer.

I can't speak for Willie, but I think *Willie and the Wheel* is Asleep at the Wheel sounding more like ourselves than any other record we've ever made. I also don't think it's coincidence that *Willie and the Wheel* happens to be our most successful crossover: the only Asleep at the Wheel album that ever made the Top 100 on the pop album charts.

Take that, MCA.

Still, I think my favorite recording with Willie is from my 2014 solo album, *A Little Piece*. The song is called "It Ain't You," and Waylon Jennings and Gary Nicholson co-wrote it not long before Waylon died in 2002. Before we got to it, "It Ain't You" had never been recorded as more than a cassette demo of just Waylon with his guitar, looking at the old guy in the mirror and saying, "That ain't me."

What that song brings home is the way youth goes away kind of right when you need it the most. You live your collective life every moment, where you might be thinking about what happened when you were five years old; or what you were trying to accomplish when you were sixteen, twenty-five, forty, sixty. Your entire life is in your mind, and when you get old, it gets crowded in there. I'm in my sixties, though I sure don't feel like it (or act like it). It's weird to do the math. Asleep at the Wheel started forty-five years ago, and going back forty-five years from then took you to 1925 and stuff like Jelly Roll Morton. That really brings home how long it's been. And yet you still feel like that kid inside you is always there.

So I was just about done with the *A Little Piece* album when my son Sam, who was co-producing the album, found "It Ain't You." Waylon had one of his biggest hits with Willie on "Luckenbach, Texas (Back to the Basics of Love)," and bringing them together again was just too perfect not to do. So Willie and I recorded it as a duet, trading verses. Just two old cats—Willie was eighty and I was sixty-two—pondering what a long, strange trip it's been.

*Soul grows young, while the body grows old.*
*Til the mind grows tired, of doin' as it's told.*
*The years fly by, we surrender to age.*
*We're like a wild bird that has chosen the cage.*
*But it ain't you, it ain't you.*
*But it's the only ride you got to get you through.*

Ain't that the truth.

# The Film Industry Is a Series of Peaks and Valleys

ASLEEP AT THE WHEEL'S run continued into 1988 with our second Grammy Award, which was also our second in the country instrumental category—*10* was the gift that kept on giving. In general, things were looking way, way up on all fronts. I had a family, two great kids. The band was as solid as it had ever been. And for the first time ever, we were financially solvent and out of debt. I hardly even knew how to act about that.

We put out another album in 1988, too—*Western Standard Time*, where we just kept on doing what we do best: Bob Wills and Ernest Tubb dance songs we all know and love, rendered with good cheer and better vibes. As we'd done on *10*, we paid tribute to another of our old Bay Area cohorts with a Western swing cover of the old 1972 Commander Cody hit "Hot Rod Lincoln." That one was even a modest hit, peaking at number 65 on the country singles charts. Video got a ton of play, too.

*Western Standard Time* wasn't the out-of-the-park smash that *10* had been, but it sold more than enough copies to make back the advance Epic had paid us. We had recouped and were earning actual royalty checks when that album won us our third country instrumental Grammy Award in the spring of 1989. What could possibly go wrong?

Epic could choose that moment to drop us, that's what could go wrong. We were stunned. But a management shake-up had pushed Rick Blackburn out in favor of Roy Wunsch. Roy was a friend of mine and we were in the black, so I figured it would be okay. But he had a new agenda that we apparently did not fit into. So despite two albums that had been hits, won Grammys, and turned a profit in a business where nine out of ten albums lose money, that was that. Of all the times that record companies have given Asleep at the Wheel a pink slip, that was the most frustrating because it made the least sense.

Once again, it was back to the drawing board.

While I embarked on another round of pavement pounding in search of a new record deal, I had other things going on, too. A Washington lawyer I knew, Howell Begle, got me in on starting up an organization dedicated to setting things right for acts—especially black acts—who had gotten ripped off in the old days. In 1987, some internal memos surfaced showing that Atlantic Records had been screwing its African American artists for decades, going back to the 1950s.

A class-action lawsuit would have taken years, with nobody but the lawyers getting paid. So a group of about a dozen of us—Bonnie Raitt, Dan Aykroyd, John Belushi's widow Judy, Texas Congressman Mickey Leland, Howard, me, and others—went to Atlantic founder Ahmet Ertegün and asked for $1.5 million to start a foundation. And that's how the Rhythm & Blues Foundation came to be. We'd do award banquets and all-star shows every year, passing out $10,000 or $15,000 checks to artists like Ruth Brown, LaVern Baker, Bobby Bland. One year, I sat between Aretha Franklin and Clarence "Frogman" Henry, and I'd swear Aretha ate two dinners that night.

It would happen the day after the Grammy Awards every year. As Little Richard put it, "The Grammys give you a nice plaque, but the R&B Foundation gives you a wall to hang it on."

I've been involved with a lot of other charity groups in Austin over the years, including the mental-health SIMS Foundation and the Health Alliance for Austin Musicians (HAAM); the Austin Community Foundation; and the St. David's Foundation, which gives out tens of millions of dollars in grants every year.

I've also been a longtime board member of public television station KLRU, which produces *Austin City Limits*. The show was on the verge of going under in the early 1990s, and it took a decade of patting backs and twisting arms, but we saved it by starting a spin-off music festival. The Austin City Limits Music Festival has become one of the biggest music events in the country, and it's helped the show survive.

Asleep at the Wheel opened the first ACL Festival in 2002, and it's become a tradition. Every year, they call and ask if we want to do it again. And every year, I say, "Hell, yes—it's the only tradition left here."

Back on the label-shopping front in 1989, we had a fortuitous turn of events when Arista Records—a label mostly known for stuff like Whitney Houston's diva pop and the elevator jazz of Kenny G—was starting up a country division, although the circumstances were peculiar. The story I heard was that Arista's head man, Clive Davis, had a "friend," Jeff Somebody, who wanted to be a country singer (this was all very hush-hush at the time, but Clive copped to being bisexual when he published his autobiography in 2013). So Clive hired Tim DuBois, a songwriter and accountant, to start Arista Nashville and his first batch of signings were Alan Jackson, Asleep at the Wheel, and Jeff. They did great with Alan Jackson, and Jeff was never heard from again.

As for us, I'd like to be able to say our time at Arista Nashville was a triumph. But the first album Asleep at the Wheel made for them, 1990's *Keepin' Me Up Nights*, did just okay, not great. We sold our usual 100,000 copies or so, got a couple more Grammy nominations, and made the label some money, but it wasn't enough. It never is. That album did have three singles that made the country charts, but none of them were any bigger than medium-sized. That drove a number-cruncher like DuBois crazy. Asleep at the Wheel presented Arista with our usual tantalizing dilemma. We were just big enough to make them think they could get something huge out of us if we'd only do some songs about piña coladas.

"I know I can get you on the radio if you'll just meet me halfway," was the way Tim put it. I knew what that really meant, and it's a conversation I've had at least a hundred times with various label types over the years. I said no thanks.

"Okay, then," Tim said, "how about a live album?"

The early '90s were also when I got back into the movie business. I'd dabbled off and on over the years, having picked up just enough film knowledge at Antioch to understand soundtrack dynamics. Peter Fonda, who'd been an Asleep at the Wheel fan since our Bay Area days, got us to do music for a late-'70s movie he did called *Wanda Nevada*, starring him and fourteen-year-old Brooke Shields. I also did the soundtracks for a late-'70s movie about pot smuggling called *Fast Money* and for *Liar's Moon*, a 1982 forbidden-love drama starring Matt Dillon that wasn't so great.

I got a better gig three years later with Horton Foote's *1918*, a wartime drama. I produced Willie and Robert Duvall doing World War I songs and became friendly enough with Duvall to keep in touch. Years later, in the early 2000s, he hired me to do a piece of music for a film in which he played an aging hit man, *Assassination Tango*. The opening scene was set in Harlem and they needed a jitterbug tune, so I wrote one called "Hoppin' with Linday." Period music is something I can do.

I've been onscreen myself a few times, too, mostly in don't-blink-or-you'll-miss-me bit parts. I played a Salt Lick barbecue pit master in the 2013 Christmas movie *Angels Sing* with Harry Connick Jr., Willie, Lyle Lovett, and a bunch of other friends. There was also this laughably bad 1996 *Thelma & Louise* knockoff called *Cadillac Ranch* that had Christopher Lloyd playing a Texas Ranger with the heaviest New York accent I've ever heard. Very possibly the worst movie of all time.

But one flick I enjoyed was *Roadie*, from 1980, which was when I really got to know Shep Gordon, the producer. We'd met years earlier when Asleep at the Wheel opened for Alice Cooper, who Shep was managing, but we bonded during *Roadie* because he's an amazing character who knows and is loved by everyone. In 2013, when the actor Mike Myers made a documentary about Shep, he called it *Supermensch*.

Shep lives in Maui these days, and visiting him is always a treat. Dinner invitations with Shep mean you'll also be dining with people like Burt Bacharach or Clint Eastwood—who had a story about once going to see Bob Wills even though he didn't like the music because "I figured there'd be some pretty girls there, and there were." Another time, we had dinner with the prince of the United Arab Emirates, who had flown in with seven girls from a modeling agency. Shep asked the prince if he knew that I was a country singer. "Oh," he asked, "do you know 'Take Me Home, Country Roads'?" I sure did. I sang it, and so did the prince—evidently the entire world knows that one by heart.

As for *Roadie*, it was a wonderful blur of personalities, and cocaine—lots and lots of cocaine. Meat Loaf starred as a truck driver turned roadie for a traveling rock show, and a bunch of musicians were in it—Peter Frampton, Alice Cooper, Roy Orbison, Hank Williams Jr., and Asleep at the Wheel. We got to play "Texas Me and You" in this scene at the Ramada Inn with Blondie and the Seven Dwarves; a tire-salesman convention was also going on, all hell was breaking loose. It's possible it didn't make sense to those who were not high. Anyway, I got an ad-libbed line in that one:

"Who booked this gig?"

As mentioned previously, we'd opted to do *Roadie* instead of *Urban Cowboy*, but at least that movie got Asleep at the Wheel a few extra gigs at some of these newly opened shit-kicker places in the early '80s. Problem was, the response we tended to get was, "That ain't what we heard in the movie." True enough, there weren't any Louis Jordan–type boogie-woogie Western swing bands in *Urban Cowboy*. Just to fuck with people, I'd sometimes put on a gold lamé turban and announce myself as "Turban Cowboy doing country-eastern music."

The crowds didn't get that, either. Oh well.

Anyway, my early-'90s foray back into film involved an actual co-starring role opposite Dolly Parton—who never did record "The Letter That Johnny Walker Read" like Leroy Preston and I wanted her to, but still became a very dear friend. First time we met, she looked up at me and said, "You're just so tall and I'm just so not. I'ma have to climb you to kiss you." She did, and I love her to death. Dolly's about four-foot-nothin', but don't be fooled by her stature, hair, or makeup.

She's a hell of a lot smarter than most people give her credit for, very quick-witted. What even fewer people know is just how hilariously coarse she can be. One time, I was talking with her about this music-convention panel discussion I was going to be on called "What Is Country?" So we were deciding what wisdom I should try to drop and I said, "We should say that country music is two cars in the yard that aren't running, and your brother's fucking your sister." Without missing a beat, Dolly said, "And your dad's jealous." Ouch, that was enough to make *me* blush.

Still, part of the charm of the whole Dolly experience is just how oblivious she can be regarding, you know . . . certain things other people notice about her, let's say. For example, the original title of the movie we did together: *Big T & the Texas Wheel*. I should mention here that my character in the movie was named Ben Rayson, and the title was the name of the band I led—yeah, a lot of imagination at work on this one. And while Dolly may have thought they were riffing on the name of my real-life band, it was going to be hard to convince the rest of the world that "Big T" wasn't a reference to Dolly's most famous attributes.

"Dolly," I said, "are you *sure* you want that title? I mean, really sure?" And she said not to worry; it would be fine, no problem. Well, that lasted until the night Dolly was on *The Tonight Show* and Johnny Carson asked what she was working on.

"A movie called *Big T & the Texas Wheel*," Dolly said, and the camera showed Carson doing his double-take thing while the crowd just roared. Only way they would've laughed louder was if it was called *Climb Every Mountain*.

So the next day, they changed the title to *Wild Texas Wind* (another real stretch). Dolly starred as Thiola Rayfield, a singer "caught in a violent, destructive relationship that leads to suspense and murder"; Gary Busey was her abusive love interest, the evil club owner Justice; and I was Ben Rayson, leader of the band Dolly/Thiola sang in and "the good guy." Willie had a bit part, too.

It was one of those TV movies of the week. Came out in 1991, and probably has not been aired since. I figured everybody in Hollywood would be calling me after that, but it didn't happen because nobody knows what to do with a six-foot-seven guy when all actors are like five-foot-four. You can only do so much with camera angles to cover that up.

Other than Gary Busey screwing up and calling me "Ray" in almost every scene, my best memory of the whole thing was the show Dolly did with Asleep at the Wheel to work out some of the music for the movie. It was at a funky outdoor joint in Austin called Liberty Lunch (which was later torn down to make way for Austin's new city hall—boo, hiss) on a cold night, and we couldn't advertise Dolly, so only a few hundred people showed up.

Dolly swept in before the show, came onto my bus, and was looking around at all my hats in there. "Yeah," she said, "this is just like my bus. Except on mine, it's wigs everywhere, not hats." Then onstage at one point, she said, "You'll have to excuse me, I'm freezing my titties off up here."

The show went great. End of the night, everybody was waving good-bye and I hollered out, "Dolly Parton, ladies and gentlemen—I'm nuts over you!"

Next day, my phone rang and it was Dolly: "I just got that joke, you son of a bitch!"

I love that woman.

# 615 Blues

ASLEEP AT THE WHEEL made that live album for Arista Nashville, *Live and Kickin'*, even though it involved the usual bullshit mind games. Ever the accountant, Tim DuBois tried to lowball us on the budget and claimed he could give us only fifty grand to make it. I wanted $75,000, which is still really cheap for a major-label project. DuBois said he'd "have to go to Clive" to get the rest, which was complete crap; $25,000 probably wouldn't even cover his tip money in Tahoe for a couple of weekends. My lawyer suggested I get someone else to make an offer to get a little bargaining power. So I concocted some subterfuge and called up good ol' Jimmy Bowen, a maverick among record men, to ask a favor.

"Jimmy," I said, "I need you to make me an offer for $75,000. It's nothing I'll hold you to, I just need to be able to tell Tim DuBois I've got an offer for that much."

Being a good egg and a mischievous sort who's not above causing trouble for the competition, Jimmy said sure, and it worked. There was much bitching from DuBois about the unfairness of it all and how I had him "over a barrel," but he coughed up the dough. We made the live album, Arista put it out, it sold enough to make a little money—and then they dropped us, just like I knew they would.

On our way out the door, I did have some conversations with DuBois about a record I'd always wanted to make. The idea was to pay homage to Bob Wills, like Merle Haggard's 1970 album *A Tribute to the Best Damn Fiddle Player in the World (or, My Salute to Bob Wills)*, which he recorded with the surviving members of Wills's Texas Playboys. And I also wanted it to be like another landmark album from the early 1970s, the Nitty Gritty Dirt Band's *Will the Circle Be Unbroken*, with lots of famous guests from different generations and genres of music.

"Well, Ray," DuBois said, "you'd better go do that one somewhere else."

Fine by me.

Back in the mid-'90s, there was a story going around Nashville about the head of a record company who declared that he wanted one of his acts to do "a duet with Patsy Cline." Great idea, boss, said the underlings. There are a lot of tracks we could use.

"No," he said, "I mean, let's do a new one." The guy did not know Patsy Cline had been dead since 1963. And while I'd like to think that story is apocryphal, I can believe it actually happened, based on my interactions with the genius captains of industry running the music industry in Nashville. There's a reason Emmylou Harris says CMA doesn't stand for Country Music Association but "Country, my ass."

Asleep at the Wheel has had some success, but to go really huge in country, you have to really—I mean, REALLY—love Jesus. And I've made a couple of Christmas albums, but it's just impossible for a Jew to appeal to the core audience because everything's about "Jesus Take the Wheel," the military coming home, and stuff like that. Go by Music Row and check the bumper stickers in the parking lots, and you'll get a pretty good idea of where the Nashville mainstream is coming from.

So what kind of town is Nashville? This kind of town: One time I was sitting next to Lee Greenwood on a plane that was about to leave. You know Lee Greenwood from *God Bless the USA*, of course. We backed him up once at the San Antonio Rodeo and it was like playing "The Star-Spangled Banner" over and over, a lot of people in the crowd yelling about killing Arabs and crap like that.

Anyway, this was the early '90s, when Billy Ray Cyrus's "Achy Breaky Heart" was the biggest thing in the world. Billy Ray's a nice guy, but I wasn't a fan of his music. So Lee Greenwood asked me what I thought of "Achy Breaky Heart" and I said it was kinda bubblegum but no big deal. And Greenwood just went off on this rant about how awful it was, just the most horrible song ever. Ten minutes later, Billy Ray himself walked onto that plane.

"This oughta be good," I thought, expecting fireworks. Instead, Greenwood went over to shake hands and tell Billy Ray how much he loved his hit, and how fantastic he thought it was.

That's the kind of town Nashville is.

Because I'm stubborn, however, I've spent a lot of years trying to play ball with Nashville. One who got away was Little Billy Gilman, who had some huge hits in the early 2000s. A friend of mine in the band Roomful of Blues discovered Billy at a state fair in Rhode Island, this nine-year-old kid with a big voice singing just spot-on karaoke. The crowd went so nuts that Roomful could not go onstage because the kid was getting mobbed for autographs afterward.

I heard Billy and thought he was incredible, so I started shopping him to Nashville. I got him hooked up with Scott Simon, Tim McGraw's manager, and he got signed to Sony Music. I'd been saying all along that I wanted to produce three cuts on Billy's album, just to show Nashville I could do mainstream music. That's what I wanted as my finder's fee, and they basically screwed me. I was cut out of it completely, which was a sore point because his first album sold two million copies.

The one crumb they gave me was to let me write and produce a song for a Rosie O'Donnell Christmas album that Billy was going to be on. So I came up with a stupid little thing called "I'm

Gonna E-mail Santa"—and it sold 500,000 copies. And afterward, of course, there was some squabbling over who owned the publishing rights. Oh, for God's sake, guys, just cut it out.

Stuff like that is just typical Nashville, a town that (piety aside) really is a den of thieves. I guess I should have known better, but so it goes. There's a famous quote that's been attributed to the late gonzo author Hunter S. Thompson: "The music business is a cruel and shallow money trench, a long plastic hallway where thieves and pimps run free and good men die like dogs." Funny thing, Hunter actually wrote that about the TV industry. And yet it applies to the record industry, too.

Meanwhile, I've got a platinum Billy Gilman record on the wall of my office. Nice that they remembered to send me one. But I'd rather have had three production credits on his album.

There's another story, about the late great bluesman Muddy Waters arriving at a recording studio and asking who the producer on the session was.

"I guess I am."

"Well, then," Muddy said, "how about you produce me a bottle of wine?"

That right there is the first rule of producing: whatever it takes. I still remember producing Darden Smith, a great singer-songwriter from Texas who I was also managing. Cleveland Chenier, older brother of zydeco legend Clifton Chenier, was also on the session. Clifton was a legend, but Cleveland was terrible on the washboard—until we got him drunk. He told us that his doctor had forbidden him from drinking brown liquor, "so bring me back a bottle of gin," he said. We did and after that, man, he was in the pocket. Sonny Landreth played guitar on that, too. A few years later, when John Hiatt was looking for a new guitarist, I hooked him up with Sonny and the Goners were born.

Producing records is problem solving with finances, logistics, transportation, and interpersonal relationships, and it requires technical, aesthetic, artistic, and psychological talents. There are technical obstacles and also artistic ones, in trying to get the person, player, or group to do what you want. Producing singers—oh my God, sometimes you have to gentle them like horses and sometimes you have to intimidate them. I've done some of both. But like I said, whatever it takes.

Early days of learning how to record, I did have some struggles. The toughest one to do was James "Slim" Hand, from Waco, one of the greatest hillbilly singer-songwriters. Lloyd Maines and I did two records with him, and they're both classic, but there was blood on those tracks. James was a troubled soul and a crazy hillbilly like Hank Williams, with all the angst and horror that implies. He had this one song called "You Can't Depend on Me" that said, "I love you but I'm a piece of shit so back off."

Now that's poetry, and he was also telling the truth. So few people do—especially in Nashville.

## *Ride with Bob*

CONFESSION TIME: Based on how huge an influence Bob Wills has always been on Asleep at the Wheel, you might think that I grew up listening to him and little else. Truth is, I didn't even hear Bob Wills until I was nearly out of high school. But once I did, I got hooked and he quickly became the musician who means the most to me, for one very simple reason: he did it all. I'd grown up playing folk music in Philadelphia with the Four G's and then gone on to jazz, blues, rock 'n' roll, fiddle tunes, country, classical, and all the rest, in and out of school. Then I heard Bob Wills's Western swing, which combined all of that and more into the most amazing music I'd ever heard, and I was smitten.

A lot of it comes down to dancing. I was at the Opry one time, talking about Bob Wills with Roy Acuff. "The difference between me and Bob Wills is he played for dances, and where I played dancing was a sin," Roy said. You know, it's like that old joke: Why don't Baptists make love standing up? Because they're afraid someone might see and think they're dancing.

"A man ahead of his time" is a phrase you hear thrown around a lot, but Bob Wills is one who earned it. He brought electric amplification, brass instruments, and drums to country music; the Grand Ole Opry never know what hit 'em the first time Wills brought his eighteen-piece band there in 1944. But afterward, everyone else on the Opry ditched their overalls for sharp-cut suits like what Wills and his Texas Playboys wore. Wills's influence was more than sartorial, too—you can still hear echoes of his Western swing today. Asleep at the Wheel blazed the revival trail, and then George Strait and Lyle Lovett were the ones who truly brought it back to mainstream popularity in the modern era.

Back in the '70s, though, breaking that stuff out sometimes confused folks. The first Bob Wills song Asleep at the Wheel covered was "Right or Wrong," in an arrangement Chris O'Connell and Danny Levin worked up to try out onstage at the Sportsman's Club in Paw Paw. But it didn't go over with the locals, who said they didn't care for "that *modern* music you're playing" and demanded we go back to "that old-time country music."

That was more than thirty years after Wills recorded the definitive 1936 Western swing version of "Right or Wrong," and West Virginia still hadn't caught up because it sounded too cool and sophisticated for the yokels there to believe we weren't doing some newfangled thing. Nope. Just Western swing, a style that never gets old and still sounds brand new.

That's why we had to move to Texas, and why we've stayed there: it's where Bob Wills is still understood. Once upon a time, Bob Wills was understood everywhere, because his style of Western swing *was* the rhythm of popular music in the 1930s and 1940s, before rhythm and blues and rock 'n' roll, and he was the ultimate rock star of his era. He was like Elvis, prancing around like a peacock in a cowboy hat at a time when most singers stood still. And he combined so many different influences, from New Orleans jazz, Mississippi blues field hollers, Mexican *gritos*—that's where he got that "Ahhh-haaa" he'd yell out. You could put Wills and his Texas Playboys on a bill with any style of music, be it blues or jazz or hillbilly or classical string quartet, and they'd fit right in and steal the audience. You couldn't ask for a better legacy to try and carry forward.

I actually met Bob Wills once, even if he didn't meet me. It was in 1973, after Asleep at the Wheel's first album came out. We started off *Comin' Right at Ya* with the Bob Wills standard "Take Me Back to Tulsa" as the very first song on side one, which was by design. Just our way of letting everybody know where we were coming from. We'd chosen that album's producer the same way; Tommy Allsup got the nod because he'd worked with Wills.

Even though *Comin' Right at Ya* didn't sell, it did kind of help get Western swing back into circulation. Tommy went to our label, United Artists Records, and convinced them it was a good idea to make another Bob Wills album. The surviving Texas Playboys would play on it with Merle Haggard singing—a big deal, because Merle was at his peak of stardom in the early '70s.

The sessions were set for two days in December 1973 in Dallas. Wills's performing career had finally ended when he had a major stroke four years earlier, and he could no longer play fiddle. But he was there on that first day to sing and do what he could for the album (which United Artists would release in 1974 as *Bob Wills and His Texas Playboys for the Last Time*).

I was invited to drop in, and the prospect of actually meeting my biggest idol was enough to make me feel like a kid in a candy store. But the experience was a grave disappointment. Bob was kind of slumped over in his wheelchair when I arrived, and we were introduced, but he wasn't really there. Bob had overtaxed himself, and his handlers said he wasn't feeling well, so they were taking him home to rest. We would try to talk the next day.

Well, that night Bob Wills had another stroke that silenced him forever. He never spoke again before he died on May 13, 1975. The night he died, Asleep at the Wheel was in Dallas and booked into the Longhorn Ballroom, a place he used to own. I'd say our set that night was a special tribute to the man and his music, but the truth is it was no more or less of a Bob Wills tribute than every Asleep at the Wheel show. That's pretty much what we do.

The same goes for our recording career. Almost every Asleep at the Wheel album has had at least one Bob Wills song, and we've also met and worked with pretty much all the surviving Texas Playboys during our history. Still, the Wills tribute I was aiming for in the early '90s would go above and beyond anything we'd done before. What I had in mind was an album of nothing but Wills tunes, with as many friends and peers doing star-turn cameos on it as possible. Just from being on the road for over twenty years, I'd made a lot of friends, and I had a lot of favors I could call in. But it really wasn't a hard sell; all my musician friends love Bob Wills, too, so it kind of sold itself.

Getting a record company to buy in on the idea was going to take a little more salesmanship, and I had just the guy in mind: the aforementioned Jimmy Bowen, who by then was head honcho at Capitol's Nashville subsidiary Liberty. Jimmy had a long and storied career going back to the 1950s, when he was in Buddy Knox's band—you know, "Party Doll." He wound up in L.A., producing albums for Sinatra, Dean Martin, and the rest of the Rat Pack, then came to Nashville and made hits with George Strait, Reba McEntire, and a bunch of others. And in the early 1990s, he had the Midas touch, thanks to Garth Brooks, who he'd helped launch into the stratosphere.

Bowen and I are simpatico for a lot of reasons, but especially because his idea of a perfect afternoon is one spent on a golf course smoking pot. Same here, so we got to be regular golfing buddies. We'd hang out, play, smoke; I might win or lose a hundred bucks, but I came out ahead either way because Bowen always paid for golf and lunch. So I picked the right moment on the golf course one day and sketched out my plan for the Wills tribute. Bowen liked it, as I knew he would.

"Let's do that," he said.

Bang, deal. We shook hands and I started working the Rolodex. Two-plus decades on, I'm still pretty proud of the lineup I got together for Asleep at the Wheel's *Tribute to the Music of Bob Wills and the Texas Playboys,* issued in 1993 on Liberty Records.

Willie, Merle, Dolly, and Vince were all on the album, of course, because how could they not be? Thirty years earlier, Bob Wills himself had written liner notes for Willie's second album, *Here's Willie Nelson* (an album featuring a few songs from the Texas Playboys repertoire and, like *Comin' Right at Ya*, produced by Tommy Allsup). And between *Salute to Bob Wills* and *For the Last Time*, Merle was one of my major inspirations for the project. All four of them are some of my dearest friends, and they were the first people I called. They all jumped at the chance.

I also got Nashville guitar legend Chet Atkins, all-around virtuoso Marty Stuart, and my fellow road dogs Riders in the Sky on it, along with that Huey Lewis fellow (which I called "the C&W debut of Huey Lewis and the Wheel" in the liner notes). I rounded up as many of the surviving Texas Playboys as I could, as well as a few Asleep at the Wheel alumni, Lucky Oceans and Chris O'Connell. Lyle Lovett and Suzy Bogguss were two rising stars I managed to catch at just the right time, on their way up.

But what put a cherry on top of it was some of the big names from the top of the charts. The timing could not have been more perfect. There was Vince Gill, who had just had his first number-one country hit, and also Garth Brooks—who once opened for Asleep at the Wheel but by then was in the midst of breaking sales records that had stood since the days of the Beatles. That's some "Deep Water," which was the song Garth sang. George Strait, another of our former opening acts who went on to headline stadiums, did "Big Ball's in Cowtown." And finally, our former Arista Nashville label mates Brooks & Dunn were on there doing "Corine, Corina," right after they'd cracked the pop Top 10 for the first time.

Seeing one of his own acts on a record he turned down might have been the last straw for poor, hapless Tim DuBois. When he saw the rest of the lineup, he just about shit a brick.

"Damn, Ray," DuBois whined, "you didn't tell me you were gonna have everybody from the Top 10 of the charts!"

"Tim," I said, "I told you all about it. But you just didn't listen."

They never do.

*Tribute* was too good to miss, and it didn't. It was Asleep at the Wheel's first album to hit the pop album charts since 1980's *Framed*, our attempted sellout. I liked this one lots better, and not just because it sold over 400,000 copies and won two Grammy Awards, including our first in a category other than country instrumental—country group with vocal, which we shared with Lyle. *Tribute* confirmed Asleep at the Wheel as rightful standard-bearers to carry on the Bob Wills legacy, which we've been proud to do. And the album did so well that it called for a sequel.

So, what the hell, we've done two sequels: *Ride with Bob* in 1999, and *Still the King: Celebrating the Music of Bob Wills and His Texas Playboys* in 2015. Same basic formula of classic Bob Wills tunes both famous and obscure plus great singers and players, mostly famous. Willie and Merle and Vince, Lee Ann Womack, Dwight Yoakam, Old Crow Medicine Show, Reba McEntire, Blind Boys of Alabama, Buddy Miller, Del McCoury, Avett Brothers, Jamey Johnson, and lots of others stepped up to contribute, some of them more than once.

I was particularly glad to have the Dixie Chicks on *Ride with Bob*, since we helped them out when they first got started. Got them signed with our booking agent, and they'd come out to open shows for Asleep at the Wheel. Early on, the Dixie Chicks' problem was that they had four harmony singers and no lead vocalist. But that problem was solved when Lloyd Maines did a session with them on steel guitar and brought along his high-school-senior daughter, Natalie. She joined, others left, and the trio version of the Dixie Chicks went on to be about the biggest thing since sliced bread.

The jury's still out on how *Still the King* will do commercially, but *Ride with Bob* did almost as well as *Tribute*, selling a quarter million copies. It also went on to win not one, not two, but three Grammys. Even picked up one for best package design, bringing Asleep at the Wheel's Grammy total over the years to nine in four different decades. Not bad.

*A Ride with Bob* was also the title of my first stage musical, which Asleep at the Wheel did in honor of what would have been Wills's 100th birthday, in 2005. I co-wrote it with Anne Rapp, a screenwriter who worked on the 1984 music-business comedy *This Is Spinal Tap* and therefore understood the intricate absurdities of the music business. We wrote it as the imagined conversation I never got to have with Bob, set on the bus during a late-night ride to Tulsa. Asleep at the Wheel's fiddle player at the time, Jason Roberts, who looks a lot like Wills, played him as a young man.

Wills's daughter hooked us up with a pretty great artifact for it, one of Bob's old cigar holders with his actual teeth marks—that's what Jason used onstage. I've got it on a shelf in my office, right next to a brick someone sent me from Main Street in Tulsa when they repaved it in front of Cain's Ballroom. On a nearby wall is a framed print of the last picture ever taken of Wills, a few hours before he had that stroke in 1973. Bill Ward, who used to run Golden West Broadcasting for Gene Autry, took it for the cover of *For the Last Time*. Before destroying the negative, he made ten prints and gave me number one.

*A Ride with Bob* was structured as me meeting Bob's ghost and then the two of us trading stories, interwoven with songs played by Asleep at the Wheel. We've done several very successful runs over the years, and we'd do more if it weren't so damn expensive to put on.

But you know, the more things change, the more they stay the same. Liberty Records was finished with Asleep at the Wheel after a couple of records and we'd moved on to another record company by the time of *Ride with Bob*, DreamWorks Records, which was the label that released it. We also did a making-of documentary to accompany that album, and after airing on PBS it won an Emmy Award in 2000.

The day after we won that Emmy, DreamWorks dropped us.

# Ride with Job

AS THE TWENTY-FIRST century dawned, Asleep at the Wheel was in a prosperous state. The band was thirty years old, and scores of players had come and gone; seemed like we'd gone through about that many record companies, too, which was one reason I started my own recording studio, to control my own means of production. But times were good—sales up, debts down, everything copacetic. Which could only mean that it was, once again, time for the whole mess to come crashing down around my ears.

This time, it was my personal life that went off the rails. I have to admit it was probably inevitable, because I've always put the band first, above everything else. Family was very important to me (and still is), but my biggest priority has always been to keep Asleep at the Wheel going. That was the deal I made with myself, that the band would come first regardless of what happened to me personally. It's why the band kept going with Chris O'Connell and me still in it, even after we broke up and she was dating the fiddle player. So I spent more than two hundred days a year on the road, because it was the only way I knew how to earn a living and support my family—but also because it's who I am. As I was about to find out, there were hidden costs to that.

Whatever the underlying causes, everything burst into the open in 2001. That was my year of living dangerously, starting with what my wife laid on me that New Year's Day. Some people start their year off by writing New Year's resolutions, but what Diane wrote was a note to me:

"I want a divorce."

WHAT?!

That had to be wrong. I blinked, shook my head, looked again—but it still said, "I want a divorce."

I'd had no idea this was coming and was completely blindsided. I would spend the next several years fighting through a breakup I didn't want, with multiple rounds of marital counseling and psychological appointments. I didn't want to put our sons through a divorce, or my band business through bankruptcy. But in the end, all my efforts went for naught.

That was strike one, my marriage.

Next thing to go was my health, right around my fiftieth birthday, when I was diagnosed with hepatitis C. I had no symptoms, but after a couple of friends with tattoos were diagnosed, I got myself checked out—and sure enough. Most likely, I got it from a tattoo in 1977 or thereabouts. One of those friends was Keith Ferguson from the Fabulous Thunderbirds, who got hepatitis from drugs and introduced it to the parlor where I picked it up. It eventually killed him.

Coming on the heels of the divorce that was supposed to be good for my marriage, the hepatitis diagnosis freaked me all the way out. I'd just turned fifty; my wife of nearly twenty years had sent me to dump city for no reason I could understand; and now I had a potentially fatal disease that could not be cured, just managed.

I did learn to manage hepatitis C, and I'm still managing it more than a decade later. Helps that I was never much of a drinker, which is just one more reason why weed is superior to booze. But it was an interesting bit of perspective to acquire, the fact that we are all just food for viruses now. Humans were just never meant to live as long as we do nowadays. I remember during marital counseling when the therapist explained that as recently as a century ago, most men didn't live much past forty, had to work sunup to sundown, and couldn't divorce because of religion. Most women, meanwhile, didn't live long enough for menopause to be an issue, and they often died during childbirth.

"So," he concluded, "we're not biologically made to survive divorce."

I didn't argue, just sighed as strike two settled into the catcher's mitt.

During those grim days of 2001, one thing that kept me going was a pending invitation to the White House. Asleep at the Wheel had played both of Bill Clinton's presidential inaugurations during the '90s, but we'd never actually played the White House. And even though I didn't vote for him, my old friend George W. Bush still invited us to come up and play what was billed as a "Bipartisan Texas Barbecue" on the South Lawn of the White House. It's something I was genuinely excited about, because Asleep at the Wheel has always been about going behind enemy lines to spread good vibes.

So we trucked on up to Washington, D.C., and checked into our hotel the evening before our White House gig. That was on September 10, 2001, and you know what happened next.

About 9:15 the next morning, September 11, David Sanger called my room, screaming, "Do you know what's happening??!!"

We spent most of that day the same way everyone else did, glued to the television and watching what seemed like the end of the world. We could walk outside and see smoke rising from the Pentagon, and the collapse of the World Trade Center twin towers was unfathomably awful to witness. Night fell, and since our gig was canceled, we decided to just get the hell out of Washington, which we could do only because we were on the bus.

So we hightailed it on out of there and rode in silence all the way to the next night's gig, playing the North Carolina Mountain State Fair. It was hard to know the appropriate thing to do, so we opened with "America the Beautiful." Considering how weird everybody felt, onstage as well as in the audience, it went about as well as it could have. But I felt a very real sense of dread taking root. Not only was my life falling apart, so was my country. And so was the entire world.

Strike three, I'm out.

One upshot of 9/11 was that it's what drove me out of Nashville once and for all. Anne Rapp and I had been working on *Stars over Texas*, a television variety series hosted by me with people like Dolly and Vince and Bruce Robison. We had some cool gimmicks, like Bruce writing a song over the course of one show based on written comments submitted by our live audience. But 9/11 shut everything down, and suddenly the only things that interested Nashville were Toby Keith, loudmouth "patriotism," hating Arabs, and dropping bombs. I love my country as much as anyone, but this was ridiculous.

Nashville has always been a very conservative place; first question everybody asks is where you go to church, and they'd always look at me funny when I'd say, "The place where all the Jews go." But 9/11 made it just unbearable. "Democrat" was a dirty word, "liberal" was worse, and God help anyone who might lean hippie. So I was out of there for good.

I was still kind of smarting over that a year or so later, when Asleep at the Wheel finally did get to play for the president at the White House; they rescheduled the barbecue and brought us back for it. There were a lot of dignitaries around—people from Congress and the Senate, a bunch of creeps from the Executive Branch, high-roller donors from Texas. Not too different from one of those long-ago nights playing down the street at Tammany Hall, in other words.

But one big difference was that this gig was outdoors, on the South Lawn of the White House. Ominous clouds were gathering overhead, and it looked like it was about to begin pouring rain at any moment. Right before we were supposed to go on, I asked Laura Bush if she was sure about this.

"Hold on," she said, and dialed a phone. She listened for a few minutes, smiled, and hung up.

"The rain will be here at 7:47," she said. "You're going on at 6:20, so you'll have plenty of time."

Just like she said, the rain held off until exactly 7:47, when the sky opened up. So, yeah, that's why people want to be president: you know exactly when it's gonna rain. Since then, they've probably figured out a way for the president to turn it on and off, too.

The image I remember most about that day was Dick Cheney sitting all by himself at a long table, just glowering. He was all hunched over his plate, glaring at people, and I was reminded of that miserable old bastard Mr. Burns from *The Simpsons*. Nobody would go near the vice president because they all seemed scared to death of him, and the impression I got was that Cheney wanted it that way. I've always thought that anybody who has no regrets and thinks they've never done anything wrong is completely full of shit, and that guy would be Exhibit A.

As someone who both leans Democrat and is a friend of George's (yes, such a thing is possible), I found it sad to watch George as president. He never seemed in control, especially after the terror attacks, and it was hard to square the person I knew with what I saw going on. He's a great guy, George is. Terrible president and not much of a politician in general, but a great guy.

I'm under no illusion that Democrats are perfect, but the ones I know seem generally more humane than the people on the other side—and also have a better sense of humor. I heard a story once about Lady Bird Johnson, LBJ's wife, driving her daughter somewhere. They saw a homeless guy begging for money on the side of the road and she pulled over to give him a dollar. Her daughter sniffed that he was probably gonna spend it on booze, and Lady Bird just shrugged.

"Honey," she said, "that might be the only medicine he gets all day."

I'm an affable sort who can tell a joke, which means I can get along with most anybody. I have no interest in going into politics myself, unlike another guy who likes to tell jokes, my old friend Kinky Friedman. I've known Kinky for years. Asleep at the Wheel was on one of his tribute records, covering "Before All Hell Breaks Loose," and that's about right. We even helped get him his first record deal. Vanguard Records was interested in Asleep at the Wheel, but we were already in good with United Artists. So I asked the three Jewish Vanguard executives who came to see us, "Have you ever heard Kinky Friedman and the Texas Jewboys?" That perked 'em right up.

So Vanguard signed Kinky and put out his first record, and he came out to open for us in Berkeley. He walked out wearing red, white, and blue chaps with a cigar and a bottle of Jack Daniel's, and the first song he did was "Get Your Biscuits in the Oven and Your Buns in the Bed." And these women's-liberation types just went crazy, storming the stage and screaming, "PIG!" I could tell Kinky was happy. I see him get the same look on his face nowadays when he's running for office and saying outrageous things. He's run for governor a couple of times, and also for agricultural commissioner on a platform of legalizing marijuana. Now that is a campaign I can get behind.

When I got "Texan of the Year," I did a list of "Top 10 Reasons Why I'll Never Run for Office." Among the reasons: "Statute of limitations hasn't run out yet"; "I'm afraid Karl Rove will swiftboat me"; and "I'll leave it to Kinky Friedman." I will, too. My only interest in politics is access. No matter which side is in power, I want to be able to deal with them so I can get stuff done.

When I'm doing the charity work for St. David's or the SIMS Foundation and need to make something happen, there's just no substitute for being on a first-name basis with people running things. At that point, whether or not you agree with (or voted for) them is immaterial. It's why Asleep at the Wheel has played inaugurations for Republicans and Democrats alike, Presidents Clinton and Obama as well as Bush. Candidate Obama even performed with Asleep at the Wheel when he was running for president the first time, getting onstage to holler a little of "Boogie Back to Texas" with us. When it comes to music, we are truly bipartisan.

But I will say that the more you're around politics, the harder it is not to turn into a jaded cynic about the whole thing. You know that saying "Politics is show business for ugly people"? It really is, and the whole thing is about money. Politicians, even the well-meaning ones, want to get friendly with rich people, and they all seem to wind up rich themselves.

If I had my way, of course, Ann Richards would have been declared queen of the universe because she was somebody I both agreed with and adored. She was a great lady, brilliant—and hilarious to be around. She came out to see us at Soap Creek Saloon when she was county commissioner, and she had to dodge five-foot-deep potholes to get there. "This road is miserable," she said, and the next day there were six trucks full of caliche filling the potholes up. Not even in her district, but she got things done.

She was unexpectedly elected governor in 1990; there's no way she would have won without her opponent screwing up—and he did. That was Clayton Williams, another pal of mine. A lot like George W. Bush: great guy, but I didn't want him for governor. We played Ann's inauguration with Willie and Dolly. My best friend, Bud Shrake, was her boyfriend.

That was fun, but being governor was hard. She'd call me up to vent, but she had the clearest assessment of political realities of anyone I've ever known. She could be brutal, too, and brutally smart. I often wonder how things might have turned out in this country if only Ann had been reelected as governor of Texas in 1994. But the tides were running against her, and she lost to George W. Bush—who used that as his springboard to becoming president, with Karl Rove pulling strings from behind the curtain.

Oh well. I don't agree with Karl Rove about much, either, but a Republican friend of mine got me a meeting with him to talk about Vietnam veterans who had hepatitis C. Nowadays, Rove is a neighbor of mine in Austin. We get along fine, long as I'm not running for office.

# *Into the Black*

BEFORE MY 2001 triple whammy, I thought I knew what depression was. I'd have little bouts here or there, but it never amounted to anything I couldn't work through, since I'm what you call a quick recycler—get depressed, get over it, all better. In retrospect, none of that was true depression. I had no fucking idea what the real thing was until 2001, when I fell into about two years of the sort of crippling depression where you can't move and just want to crawl into the nearest hole, curl up, and die. It was beyond horrible. That's the problem with depression—you think you'll never enjoy life again.

Divorce proceedings dragged on into a war of attrition, but I got to where I barely noticed, because I was inside my own head so much of the time. The hepatitis turned me into the worst sort of hypochondriac, convinced that every cough was cancer. Meanwhile, the rest of America sank into insanity as we blundered into a stupid war that anybody could tell was a bad idea.

Through all of it, however, I had one bright spot: music. That was the only thing that kept me from completely losing my damn mind. Even at my lowest point, when I could not drag myself out of bed for anything else, I could still get on the bus and go do a show. And as soon as I was onstage and under the lights, everything else went away. Depression can be a learning experience, and a creative one if you have an outlet like music. It can kill you, or sustain you, or even both. I was listening to a piece of classical music the other day, and it was so obvious that the guy who wrote it was sad as could be, it brought tears to my eyes.

It was a good thing that I got cash as well as comfort out of playing music, because I had to keep right on working no matter what. I didn't even get a lawyer because I just did not have the will to fight her.

"Whatever you want," I told Diane, "I'll sign. Just don't ruin my business."

She took a hell of a lot of money, but she did leave the business more or less intact—just saddled with debts as deep as my depression. Climbing out of both those holes would take years of struggle. Asleep at the Wheel was back to scuffling, just like the early 1980s all over again. Worse, even. The band went down to five pieces, and at one point we even had to go out without a steel player, which might be the only time in the last thirty years that I've missed Junior Brown.

Nothing like divorce to make you write like crazy, and I did. Then a guy from Koch Records came to me and said, "I just want to tell you, Ray, that you've done more with less talent than anyone I've ever met. We want you to make a solo album."

Well, now, that's got to be the worst backhanded compliment ever, but I was happy to spend his money. They told me to do whatever I wanted, so I got Dolly, Delbert McClinton, and even jazz guitarist Stanley Jordan.

That was *Beyond Time*, the solo album I made in 2003. Didn't sell all that well, but it did pick up two Grammy nominations. Making my first record outside the confines of Asleep at the Wheel was an attempt to stretch out a bit and try other things. But there's also no denying that I wasn't feeling much like a party around then. So a moody divorce record where every song was basically "you bitch," with late-night jazz arrangements, seemed musically as well as emotionally honest.

That especially went for "Isn't It Strange?," an old song I'd written twenty-five years earlier that just never fit Asleep at the Wheel. But it sure did fit my life in 2003. So I dusted it off:

*Isn't it strange?*
*I guess that's the way true love ends.*
*Isn't it strange?*

I'll say. Anne Rapp, my co-writer on *A Ride with Bob*, once told me that I always look like I just "glide through everything like it never happened." While I'm glad that was the outward appearance, inside me was a lot of turmoil, anger, sadness, and depression. I dealt with it as best I could, in fits and starts with a lot of backsliding.

Diane and I made one last attempt to patch things up. I told myself she was a good person, I'd loved her, she'd done a great job raising our sons—and all of that was true. But it was too late and I'd lost trust. Not that I was anything like trustworthy myself around that time. There was a nebulous period where I was seeing multiple women at the same time, one of whom was Diane, and it ended pretty much just how you'd expect—badly, with everyone mad at each other.

Finally, I told Diane I just couldn't do it anymore and we were done. And right around then, I started seeing a woman named Michelle Valles. She was thirty-one years old (twenty-five years younger than me), a TV reporter, and beautiful enough to stop traffic. That's when the war really started.

Before the divorce, Diane and I lived in a nice house on three acres in the hills west of Austin, a parcel that would be worth a scary fortune today. I kept the house, but Diane insisted on splitting the lot in half and building a house of her own right next door.

So I put up a nine-foot fence between my house and hers, because good fences make good neighbors.

Michelle and I were together for about seven years, and I was just crazy in love with her the whole time. But we finally came to the end of the road over several things. For one thing, she wanted kids; mine were grown and I felt like I was just too old to start over. Then Michelle moved up the ladder from Austin to a major-market station in Los Angeles in 2012, so that's when we split up.

It was very amicable and nothing at all like my divorce, but still difficult. And since solo albums seem to be how I deal with my big breakups, I put out another one in 2014. It was called *A Little Piece*, and I didn't even realize just how personal it was until after I'd finished it. I played a few cuts off it for Elizabeth McQueen (who was then the Wheel's female singer), and she said, "That's really dark."

True enough. I'd written those songs as an emotional release, because it's how I process things, even though that's a fine line. I remember some years ago a singer coming to me with an album of songs he'd done, and he asked what I thought. And the songs were just so blatantly personal, they were almost embarrassing to hear.

"You have to write about feelings in a way others can relate to," I told him. I never wanted to be that guy who puts enough personal stuff out there to make people cringe.

But I was kind of moving in that direction after a project called *Poet*, a Townes Van Zandt tribute album that had come out in 2001. That was during my bad year, and Asleep at the Wheel did "If I Needed You," a song that really spoke to me:

*If I needed you*
*Would you come to me*
*And ease my pain? . . .*

Doing that song and seeing people respond, I started feeling like I could do some really personal songs of my own outside Asleep at the Wheel's good-time party stuff. So after my breakups with Diane and Michelle, I ended up writing a bunch of songs about mortality and looking back. Found a few songs like that by other people, too, like Waylon's "It Ain't You."

Michelle gets some credit for the title song, too. "A Little Piece" has a message that you should avoid doing anything that might make you "lose a little piece of you." I'd never completely finished it, or even played it for anyone else, because it felt almost nakedly personal. Then I played what I had so far for Michelle, and she insisted that it was one I had to finish. She was right, of course.

*I know a little about a lot of things that is true*
*One thing I know, what you give comes back to you.*

I may not always live up to that, but I sure do try.

# *Epilogue*

## BRINGING IT ALL BACK HOME

MANY YEARS AGO, Asleep at the Wheel was booked into a place in Louisiana called the Old South Jamboree. Didn't know a thing about it until our bus pulled up and we saw a twelve-foot-tall iron cross. Turned out the Old South Jamboree really was an Old South kind of place, as in a meeting hall for the local Ku Klux Klan. So there we were, a band with three Jews, two Catholics, and one black man as far as the Klan would be concerned—Tony Garnier's dad is Creole and his mom is an American Indian.

The sheriff from the parish was there talking about how he loved Asleep at the Wheel and saying, "Bob Wills is the best." The Bob Wills song he and his Klan pals liked the most was "Take Me Back to Tulsa," which has a line about how "dark man picks the cotton, white man gets the money." That made those guys think, "Right on!" I asked the sheriff about the big iron cross, and he said, "We got tired of messing with the wooden ones, so we just drape this in burlap, throw on some gas, and light it!" And that's what they did.

So Tony tucked his Afro under his hat and stayed out of the lights as best he could, and I tried to Jew it down as best I could. We did the show—as I remember, "Take Me Back to Tulsa" went over particularly well—and got the hell out of there. I don't think anybody on the bus exhaled until we were at least ten miles down the road.

I'll tell you, though: as bad and weird as that scene was, it sure was memorable, and that's kind of what keeps me going. People ask how I can still be out there after all these years, riding the bus and playing the same songs, telling the same jokes. Are you kidding? It's never the same, and it's always interesting.

We've played gigs for $40,000 and gigs for free (and a lot more freebies than forty-grands, let me tell ya), and no two have been alike. We've opened for legends in some of the finest rooms on earth and for a troupe of dancing molars, toothbrushes, and vegetables at "The World's Largest Free Fair" in Bogalusa, Louisiana. That's one freaky state, Louisiana. We've played Cajun places there when we were in one room and cockfights were going on in another.

Forty-some years ago, we went off to look for America. I think we found it, in all its good, bad, ugly, and kooky glory. Asleep at the Wheel doesn't really fit in anywhere and never has. But the upside of not fitting into any one place is that we kind of fit in everywhere. That's given us the opportunity to do some incredibly weird and wonderful things over the years. One of our strangest-ever collaborations was with a leaf player from China. When you were a kid, did you ever blow on blades of grass to make a kind of scraggly noise? This guy turned that into music. We sent him a tape of "Miles and Miles of Texas" and he brought in a tree branch, selecting just the right leaf for that song's key, and he blew the tune with us while about twenty Chinese dancers whirled around for cameras that filmed the whole spectacle. It was as freaky a thing as I have ever done, and that's saying a lot. I gave all those dancers Asleep at the Wheel CDs to take home, and I have no idea what people there thought of them—or of "Miles and Miles of Texas" played on a leaf when it aired on Chinese television. But as weird-ass musical diplomacy goes, that's pretty cool.

One of the few brushes with history we ever turned down was in 1978, when the notorious British punk band the Sex Pistols came through Texas. The promoters wanted regional openers—Cajun bands in Louisiana, blues in Chicago, and us in Texas.

Good intentions, but still a bad idea. All their opening acts got pelted with beer bottles and abused, so we said no thanks. Their kind of punk rock was never my thing anyway.

But pretty much everything else, we've said yes to. We've not only played "Boogie Back to Texas" with President Obama, but on *Brady Bunch* star Florence Henderson's cooking show and even with a football player—New York Giants cornerback Jason Sehorn did it with us on the 1996 album *NFL Country*. We've done two Christmas albums even though I'm Jewish, because between Jesus and Irving Berlin, there would be no Christmas without Jews. And over the years, we've opened for Alice Cooper, James Brown, the Hues Corporation ("Rock the Boat"), and Jimmy Cliff while recording with everything from symphony orchestras to Tejano bands. And that Chinese leaf player.

What might be weirdest of all is that everything seems to work. "I don't like country, but I like you guys" is something we hear repeatedly, pretty much night in and night out. Hey, boogie-woogie Western swing is hard not to like.

So we'll just keep riding that wave.

Personal romantic travails aside, the last decade has been a good one for Asleep at the Wheel. People have continued coming and going, of course, but we just reload, replace, and keep on. Elizabeth McQueen did a nice long stretch as our female vocalist before bowing out to raise her kids in 2014, and she was replaced by Katie Shore, a very fine singer and fiddle player. Elizabeth's husband, David Sanger, is still our drummer; having been on board since 1986, he's the second-longest-running member of the band behind yours truly.

It took a few years for us to recover financially, but we finally got our mojo back and got out of debt, building Asleep at the Wheel back up to a thriving enterprise again. We do about a million dollars' worth of business a year (even though we spend about a million-two to do it, har har), bringing the gospel of Bob Wills to honky-tonk dance floors worldwide. We're also into recording and management. After decades of making records for labels large and small, we finally took all that in-house and started handling pretty much every step of the process ourselves.

My recording studio and label are both called Bismeaux, named after a rabbit-like character from the 1950s comic strip *Pogo*. I just like the sound of it. In 2010, Asleep at the Wheel put out an album on Bismeaux Records called *It's a Good Day*, and it was. Sold enough copies to make number 57 on the country charts. Bismeaux even won record label of the year for 2014 in the *Austin Chronicle*'s Austin Music Awards. Somehow, everything seems to work out enough to keep the whole enterprise moving forward.

Pondering this autobiographical journey, I'm humbled to still be alive and well and even relatively well-off. For forty-five years, I've been able to travel the world and play music with such a talented, dedicated band of musical brothers and sisters, and we're still going strong. And if it hasn't always been easy, well, easy wasn't what I signed up for all those years ago. So much has happened, which is why I'm finally putting out this book after spending so many years writing down what I could remember—what I was thinking, doing, and trying to accomplish, not to mention who I was hangin' out with and what all was goin' on. A lot, man.

In my lifetime, I've seen segregation and the civil rights era; Vietnam, the Cold War, and the breakup of the Soviet Union and the Iron Curtain; and Iran, Iraq, Afghanistan, and, of course, 9/11. There have been cataclysmic changes all over the world. And with all that going on, I've been lucky enough to stay on my musical path and realize not just goals but dreams. Everyone should be as lucky as I've been.

Both my sons have grown up to be fine, upstanding men. Younger brother Aaron works as a film editor in Hollywood, where he cuts movie trailers. He did the trailer for 2012's *Silver Linings Playbook*, a movie that won an Oscar. He's got a job and he's not hitting me up for money, and that right there is parental paradise.

As for Aaron's big brother, Sam, he's my heir apparent if he wants to be. He was an all-state golfer in high school and pursued that for a while before gravitating to music and getting the recording bug. Nowadays, he's the studio manager at Bismeaux, where he runs sessions and does an excellent job at it. As I told him, "The good news is you're working for me, and that's the bad news, too." But he's turned into a great producer. He co-produced *A Little Piece* for me with Lloyd Maines. I'm proud of that record, and of both my boys.

The way things stand now, Asleep at the Wheel cannot exist without me. There's been only one Wheel show where I didn't play, in Corpus Christi years ago; I was sick as a dog and couldn't go on, and it was a disaster. I won't be around forever, obviously, and what happens when I'm gone is up to Sam. He's a great guitar player, he sings like me, and he's got the talent. Whether or not he'd want to be a bandleader is something he'll have to decide. Either way, I figure he'll keep the studio going. But I'm not worried.

Hell, friends, I'm not worried about much. Chris O'Connell has said that the dream of all the Western swing guys is to go out with their boots on, in the spotlight onstage, which sounds about right. I make jokes about that—"Don't worry about me, folks, I'm gonna die in front of a thousand people!"—but death is a part of life and it will someday get us all. So I make jokes about it, and I try to make the most of every day. I hope you do, too.

Well, that's pretty much it for now, even though there's plenty more I could tell you. Come see me sometime and I'll tell it in person, because we'll be coming through your town soon. But right now, it's about time for me to get back on the bus.

Meantime, I hope you enjoyed this trip down memory lane as much as I did. We'll see you on down the road.

# Acknowledgments

TO CHRIS O'CONNELL, Floyd Domino, and all the rest of the hundred-plus musicians and many more roadies, engineers, producers, agents, managers, publicists, publishers, promoters, and everyone else who rode, drove, or pushed the bus, manned the phones, answered the e-mail, hauled the gear, cut the tape, and helped keep the Wheel rollin' over the past four and a half decades—thank you, thank you, thank you.

But thanks most of all to Reuben "Lucky Oceans" Gosfield and Leroy Preston, my original partners in crime, without whom none of this would have been possible. Great friends as well as world-class musicians, they were my companions in an adventure most were too afraid to join in on. I'm more grateful than I can say that you took the leap with me. And I should probably also thank Lee and Larry Sigler, who let us stay at that cabin in the West Virginia wilderness, the one where the whole saga began all those years ago.

To the millions of fans over the years who have shown up to listen, dance, and encourage (or heckle) us through good times and bad, I thank you from the bottom of my soul. You have been the air that I breathe. All of us tonight, we are Asleep at the Wheel.

From Commander Cody to Van Morrison, Willie Nelson to Dolly Parton, Emmylou Harris to George Strait, the Doobie

Brothers and Huey Lewis to Dan Hicks and the Hot Licks, Vince Gill to Lyle Lovett and so many more—your help and support have meant the world to me. Thank you.

I'd also be remiss if I didn't thank the journalists and writers who have been so good to Asleep at the Wheel over the years: Ed Ward, John Morthland, Nick Tosches, Bill Holland, and many others who chronicled us and let the world know what we were trying to do. Thanks also to David Menconi, my co-writer, for his patience and diligence.

To Mike Seifert, Ann Richards, Jerry Wexler, Del Shannon, Stevie Ray Vaughan, Peter Sheridan, Waylon Jennings, Bob Wills, and everyone else in this tale who is no longer with us—rest easy, friends.

Finally, to the best family a man could hope to have: Mom and Dad, sons Sam and Aaron (the best thing that ever happened to me), brothers Mike and Hank and sister Sandy—the greatest siblings ever. And while I'm at it, I'll quote Willie and send a shout-out "To All the Girls I've Loved Before." This book's for all y'all.

So here it is, the story of a second-generation Jewish kid from Philadelphia who loved it, learned it, and lived it, willing himself to become a country star. If I'm not the American dream . . . well, sir, at least I did the soundtrack.

—Ray Benson
Austin, Texas

Gratitude and appreciation to Martha Burns and the Menconi kids—Aaron, Edward, and Claudia—for support, encouragement, and being all-around good sports; to Casey Kittrell and Dave Hamrick at University of Texas Press for putting me on the trail; to Jan and Larry Byrd for catering, accommodations, and transportation at my Austin home away from home; to Peter Schwarz, Sam Seifert, David Sanger, Elizabeth McQueen, Milkdrive, Joan Myers, MJ, PJ, Mack, and the rest of the Asleep at the Wheel crew for graciously welcoming me into their world; to Vince Gill and Amy Grant for maybe the best barbecue I've ever had outside of Texas; to Ed Ward and Joe Nick Patoski for advice both good and prescient; and to Dave Rose, Barry Poss, Peter Blackstock, Gil Asakawa, Leland Rucker, Steve Knopper, and, of course, Scott Huler for a steady supply of those ever-important good vibrations.

Finally, to the man himself, Ray Benson, I'd like to send out a few of Bob Wills's *grito* whoops. It's been an honor, privilege, and pleasure to help you tell this story. *Ah ha ha!* . . .

—David Menconi
Raleigh, North Carolina

# Discography

*Comin' Right at Ya*, United Artists Records, 1973
*Asleep At The Wheel*, Epic Records, 1974
*Texas Gold*, Capitol Records, 1975
*Wheelin' and Dealin'*, Capitol Records, 1976
*The Wheel*, Capitol Records, 1977
*Collision Course*, Capitol Records, 1978
*Served Live*, Capitol Records, 1979
*Drivin'*, Imperial House Records, 1980
*Framed*, Capitol Records, 1980
*Pasture Prime*, MCA-Dot, Demon and Stony Plain Music, 1985
*Asleep At The Wheel: 10*, Epic Records/CBS, 1987
*Western Standard Time*, Epic Records/CBS, 1988
*Keepin' Me Up Nights*, Arista Records, 1990
*Live & Kickin' (Greatest Hits)*, Arista Records, 1992
*Tribute to the Music Of Bob Wills and the Texas Playboys*,
Liberty Records, 1993
*Swing Time*, Sony Records, 1995
*The Wheel Keeps On Rollin'*, Capitol Records Nashville, 1995
*Back to the Future Now: Live at Arizona Charlie's, Las Vegas*,
Epic Records/Lucky Dog Records, 1997
*Merry Texas Christmas, Y'all*, High Street Records, 1997
*Ride With Bob*, DreamWorks Records, 1999

*The Very Best of Asleep at the Wheel*, Relentless Nashville, 2001
*Hang Up My Spurs*, Cracker Barrel Heritage Series, 2002
*Texas Fiddle Man*, Jason Roberts, Bismeaux Records, 2002
*Asleep at the Wheel Live at Billy Bob's Texas*, Smith Music, 2003
*Asleep at the Wheel Remembers the Alamo*, Shout! Factory, 2003
*Beyond Time*, Ray Benson (Solo), Audium/Koch, 2003
*Live in Concert*, InAkustik, Germany, 2003
*Wave on Wave*, Pat Green, Universal Records, 2003
*A Heart Wide Open*, Tish Hinojosa, Valley Records, 2005
*Mad Dogs & Okies*, Jamie Oldaker, Concord Music Group, 2005
*The Best of Asleep at the Wheel on the Road*, Asleep at the Wheel, Madacy Entertainment, 2006
*Dang Me*, Willie Nelson & Jack Ingram, Cracker Barrel, 2006
*Hillbilly Shakespeare*, Eugene Chrysler, Dan Karlok, Carclo Records, 2006
*Live at Austin City Limits*, Asleep at the Wheel, New West Records, 2006
*Reinventing the Wheel*, Asleep at the Wheel, Bismeaux Records, 2006
*San Angelo*, Aaron Watson, Big Label Records, 2006
*Santa Loves to Boogie*, Asleep at the Wheel, Bismeaux Records, 2006
*The Truth Will Set You Free*, James Hand, Rounder Records, 2006
*Why The Hell Not, The Songs of Kinky Friedman*, Various Artists, Sustain Records, 2006
*Always Lift Him Up: A Tribute to Blind Alfred Reed*, Various Artists, Proper Records, 2007
*Lucky Steels the Wheel*, Lucky Oceans/Asleep at the Wheel, LOCD, 2007
*With the Fort Worth Symphony Orchestra*, Asleep at the Wheel, Bismeaux Records, 2007
*Angels and Outlaws*, Aaron Watson, Big Label Records, 2008
*Miss Understood*, Carolyn Wonderland, Bismeaux Records, 2008
*Willie and the Wheel*, Willie Nelson & Asleep at the Wheel, Bismeaux Records, 2009

*Celebrating with Friends*, Johnny Gimble, CMH Records, 2010
*It's a Good Day*, Asleep at the Wheel and Leon Rausch, Bismeaux Records, 2010
*Sinners & Saints*, Raul Malo, Fantasy Records/Concord Music Group, 2010
*Texas Songbook*, Gary Nicholson, Bismeaux Records, 2011
*Deep In The Heart: Big Songs For Little Texans*, Various Artists, Bismeaux Records, 2012
*Living for a Song: Tribute to Hank Cochran*, Jamey Johnson, Mercury Records, 2012
*Tim McGraw & Friends*, Tim McGraw, Curb Records, 2013
*A Little Piece*, Ray Benson, Bismeaux Records, 2014
*Songs from a Stolen Spring*, Multi-lingual Duets, Valley Entertainment, 2014
*Still The King: Celebrating the Music of Bob Wills and his Texas Playboys*, Asleep at the Wheel, Bismeaux Records 2015

# Index